PONGO
The Rescue Horse

★ **Chapter 1** ★

D1598923

Leigh Moves To Horse Country

Leigh was nine years old when she moved with her parents to their Granny's old home in the country in eastern Virginia. Leigh always used to stay at Granny's country house when she came to visit, and she remembered behind her Granny's house there were beautiful horses in a big pasture. Leigh would sit by the sunny back window with her Granny and watch the horses graze.

Granny would make homemade chocolate pudding and they would enjoy the beautiful view of the neighbor's pastures, wood fences and pretty barn. Leigh would watch the swishing tails and glistening coats off the horses as they slowly chomped on green grass. Sometimes Granny would read her a story as they sat in her cozy kitchen and glanced out the back window now and then. If the weather was nice, Granny would take her by the hand and they would walk up close to the fence where the horses were. As a little girl, Leigh would look up at the horses from the fence and feed them apples or Granny's homemade oatmeal treats. She remembered the horses seemed so huge as they propped their heads over the fence sniffing down at her. Their giant mouths gently taking a treat from her tiny hand.

Those were special memories in her early childhood. This trip up to Virginia would be different though, her family got the news that Granny had gone to heaven. Granny's house was now going to be their house. Granny and the family wanted them to have it, so they could all live closer to each other. It was a wonderful blessing, but they would all miss sweet Granny very much.

Leigh, her Mom and Dad packed up the moving truck from their rental house in Carolina. Dad drove the moving truck with their dog Junior in the front seat and Mom and Leigh drove behind in the family car. It was bitter-sweet seven hour ride up to Virginia from North Carolina. She was sad about not being able to see Granny anymore, but excited about moving to the country - horse country.

Every year, when Leigh would come up to Virginia to visit, she would go to the Spring Strawberry Festival, riding the rides, eating strawberry shortcake and most of all getting a chance to ride a horse at the Festival! She would pet their soft noses and look in their big gentle eyes. It was so amazing to sit up high on a horses back. She would hang on tight to the saddle horn as they led the horse around in a circle. Even though the horse ride only lasted a few minutes, Leigh took in every second, imagining how wonderful it would be to be able to ride all the time. Leigh loved horses. She felt like she could understand them, better than she could understand people.

Now, years later she was moving to this beautiful horse country to stay! As Leigh and her family arrived in Virginia with the big moving truck, they traveled down the country roads near her new home and passed by all the white fenced farms, with horses and ponies contentedly roaming in the green pastures.   She wondered why God had brought her and her family to this horse country?   What could be in store for her future here?

She put a hope in her heart that her parents could buy her the horse of her dreams someday that would be her best friend.

Soon, they had all their furniture moved into Granny's house. Leigh could not wait to walk behind the house and down the lane with her Mom and go feed the neighbor's horses carrots and pet them. These were the same horses that she used to go visit with Granny over the years. Leigh wondered what it would be like to have a fence and a barn at her house, a home for her own horse! Oh, what a wonderful day it would be when she could just look out her bedroom window and there was *her horse* right there in her own yard!

As the months went by, Leigh would walk down the lane behind her house to where the horses were. Her neighbor, known as "Miss Bridgett" owned the farm, and she did not mind having Leigh visit the horses almost every day. Miss Bridgett's horses were retired show horses, nobody rode them anymore. They were very gentle.

Big Mikey was a big bay thoroughbred who would come down and graze in the pasture that connected to Leigh's backyard. Leigh would go and sit in the grass next to the fence and talk to Big Mikey as he would nibble on carrots that she handed to him between the fence rails. She loved the summertime where she could go out there and spend the day climbing trees and looking over the pastures. She would imagine herself riding and galloping across the green grass with her very own horse. Her afternoons chatting with Big Mikey were sweet, but then it was time for Leigh to go to school. She hoped that she could meet other kids who liked horses too!

✭PONGO✭
The Rescue Horse

★ **Chapter 2** ★

True Friends Look At The Heart

Leigh was a shy and quiet girl. School days were hard sometimes. She loved learning in school and really liked all her teachers, but there were some mean kids who would tease her all the time. She tried to make friends, but was afraid to do group things in class because these same mean kids would try to embarrass her. She thought she was a nice person, her Mom and dad told her she was smart and pretty, but the mean kids made her feel bad about herself. They made fun of her clothes and her glasses and braces on her teeth, pushed her out of her seat on the bus and stole her cookies at lunch. She was trying to be kind to them, but they would not stop doing mean things. She was very lonely, sad and tired of being bullied.

The only friend she had all the time was Big Mikey the horse. She could come home off the school bus and go back to the pasture connecting to her backyard talk to the big old Thoroughbred about her day. Big Mikey always listened and accepted her just as she is. She would stroke his brown nose through the fence and he would stand there and listen to her for hours, swishing his tail back and forth and flicking his ears, stopping to chomp on a carrot here and there. This was always something Leigh looked forward to - her time with Big Mikey the horse. He helped her get through the hard days more than he knew.

As Leigh got older, she started Middle School. For Leigh it was just a bigger school with more kids and more bullies unfortunately. Leigh tried to avoid the bullies in the lunchroom and in the hallways and on the bus. She thought if she stayed quiet and to herself - maybe they would leave her alone. She felt like she wanted to be invisible.

Leigh enjoyed writing stories and poems, and wrote in her journal often. She thought if she could just hide behind her books, the bullies would not bother her. She tried that on the bus, and two girls started calling her "old library lady", and another boy kept trying to steal her journal out of her hands as she was writing in it. He grabbed it and started reading out loud to everyone her private things she wrote in her journal and laughed and mocked her. Then he only gave it back after the bus driver yelled at him.

One day it was just too much. That afternoon Leigh got off the school bus completely worn out from all the name calling and teasing she received from the bullies all the way home for a 30 minute bus ride. She came in the front door of her house, threw her back pack on the chair and laid down in the middle of the carpet - just no more energy to even make it to her room. Mom came in and was baffled. "Leigh, are you Ok sweetheart?" Mom asked in a worried tone.

"Oh, Mom, why are people so mean? I just don't understand why the kids at school constantly want to make fun of me." Leigh replied. "Today, I had really hard day. I had gym class today, I could not keep up with the running on the track with the other kids. I did not want to stand out by being the slowest person because I knew it would just be another reason for the mean girls in my gym class to say something hateful to me. Uggggg!!" She groaned.

"I am so sorry, sweetheart." Mom said trying to console her.

Leigh continued; "I feel like no matter what I do I just can't get away from the bullying, it's like I am a target or something. I JUST DON'T GET IT!" Leigh threw her hands up in frustration.

"I know that I am a nice person, maybe not most popular or in sports." Leigh explained. "But Mom, I don't want to keep going to the teachers or the guidance counselors all the time, because they always ask me *who* is bullying me, and if I tell them, then those kids get in trouble, and then those same kids just come after me even worse." Leigh leaned up against the couch and hugged her knees tightly. Tears welling up in her eyes, she was in complete despair.

Mom then explained to her that kids can be mean because they don't yet understand that God made each of us unique and for a special purpose. Sometimes those kids don't have a happy life at home, and they are acting out their anger at school on other kids. Many times these same kids that 'bully' actually are very afraid themselves, and put on a mean attitude to pretend they are tough.

Leigh thought about that for a minute. That could be true, but then why didn't the other kids like her? Why could they not see that she had a kind heart? Leigh learned in the Bible that God looks at the heart of a person and not what they look like or clothes they wear. Leigh liked the clothes she wore and she saw nothing wrong with wearing glasses or having braces. Why did she not fit in with the other kids? She was confused and really tired from dealing with all of it. It was affecting her school work and grades.

Sometimes she would get a stomach ache from being worried about facing the bullies each day and she did not even want to go to school. Leigh kept trying to ignore the bullying. But the same kids kept bullying her, with the same old stuff every day. They made fun of her clothes and her glasses and braces on her teeth, pushed her out of her seat on the bus and stole her cookies at lunch, One time she even tried to bring brownies for lunch and they took them, too!

By the time Leigh came home each day all she wanted to do was cry. Leigh's Mom and Dad went to the school and spoke to her teachers and even the principal. They all wanted to help Leigh, but if Leigh would not tell them who the bullies were, they could not help her very much. Leigh did not want to tell because she knew if she did those same bullies would come against her even more when the teachers were not around.

Leigh was a smart girl, and her teachers loved her and she loved to learn. She was so frustrated that she could not enjoy school because of the sneaky bullies. There had to be a way to get through her Middle School years in peace. "Please God," Leigh prayed through tears. "Help me through this, God, Please give me a true friend who likes me for who I am and will stand by me, no matter what, Amen."

A few weeks later, when Leigh came home off the school bus, she asked her Mom if she could do homeschooling for a while so she could get away from the bullying. She really needed a break. She had been researching homeschooling on her own, as a possible option to take some time away from public school. Her Mom said OK we will give it a try if she could get her classes online and all the credits she would need for 7th and 8th grade.

Leigh went on her computer and gathered all the research for homeschooling online to present to her parents. She was determined to be able to take a break from public school to get away from the bullies. Mom was impressed with all her research. They sat down and made the decision for Leigh to do homeschool for a while, until she was ready to go back to public school. They went ahead and enrolled that day online! The next day, for the first time in a long time, Leigh got up in the morning excited to begin a school day - on her computer! Her Mom had waffles ready for her and she could do her studies in her pajamas! Mom was there to help if she got stuck plus she could ask questions of her online teachers. It was a very cool deal!

During the day, Leigh could even go out back and visit Miss Bridgett's horses any time she wanted to take a break. Big Mikey had been getting older and more feeble, and was mostly staying close by the barn. Leigh would walk up the lane to the barn spend time with him. He was always happy to see her, nickering to her as he saw her approaching. Rubbing his head on her arm as he knew she had carrots in her pocket. Leigh enjoyed having more freedom to do what she wanted, but she also had to make sure she got her homeschool assignments handed in daily. Her parents were proud of her, and she was too. She even helped Mom cook dinner, or if she wanted she could just heat up a pizza in the oven when Mom was busy in her office.

Leigh still just wanted some of her own friends to accept her for who she was and see that she could be a good friend too! Hanging with Big Mikey made the days brighter - and she was so relieved that she did not have to deal with bullies anymore.

One winter day, Leigh and her Mom came home from the store, Leigh happened to glance back at Miss Bridgett's place and could not see Big Mikey anywhere, not even up by the barn. Leigh got worried about her old friend. When they got in the house, Mom called Miss Bridgett to ask her if everything was OK. Leigh heard her Mom say, "Oh Miss Bridgett we are so sorry! Is there anything we can do?" Leigh knew it was bad news. Her Mom hung up the phone, and said with a deep sigh, "Leigh, I have sad news.... Big Mikey is gone.... he died this afternoon, I am so sorry sweetheart, I know you were very fond of him."

Leigh felt like someone had kicked her in the stomach. All she been through and now this. She quietly went to her room, laid down and cried on her pillow. Her Mom came in and sat on the end of her bed. "Leigh," Her Mom said gently. "I know you are very sad. This news is hard to take, we will miss seeing Big Mikey out back. But Miss Bridgett is very sad to lose Big Mikey too, she had him for a long time. He was her horse and she loved him." Leigh looked up at her Mom, wiped her tears and thought for a moment - and after swallowing hard she said; "Mom, can we get Miss Bridgett a card and tell her we are sorry about Big Mikey and let her know how much happiness he brought us and Granny over the years?"

"I think that would be a wonderful thing to do." Said Mom. "You truly have a beautiful heart, Leigh. I know Miss Bridgett will be comforted to hear how Big Mikey was a friend to so many of us."

Leigh and Mom found the perfect card at the store the next morning with a picture of a horse grazing in a misty pasture. They sat down together and wrote out a message to Miss Bridgett, thanking her for sharing Big Mikey with all of them and what a good friend he was. Leigh sealed up the envelope and drew a picture of Big Mikey in pencil on the back of the envelope and addressed the card to Miss Bridgett. She ran to the mailbox and set it in there. She hoped Miss Bridgett would feel better about losing Big Mikey after she read the card. She felt better just to be able to send the card. It felt good to know that she could at least do something to help the empty space Big Mikey left when they all looked out to the pasture - and he was no longer there, ready to come to the fence and happily munch on carrots.

That night Leigh could not sleep. Her mind would not be quiet. Even though she was doing well in homeschool, she was still very lonely. Horses had brought her so much joy, and she missed Big Mikey already. She was shy about doing things around kids and other people. But she enjoyed being around her pets and animals. She was comfortable around them. Sometimes she would go to a youth event at church and she just felt like she was not confident enough to take part in group activities. She needed more time to learn how to become more sure of herself. It was really hard to trust new kids to be her friends, since she had been so hurt by the mean kids who had bullied her in the past.

So many times in her young life, she felt like God was passing her by - that maybe He did not really hear prayers or even care about her. She had been rejected by the mean kids that she was just trying to be friends with. Then Big Mikey passing away. "Life is so hard and cruel!" Leigh thought aloud as she laid awake looking at the ceiling.

One thing Leigh did know for sure was she wanted to do more with horses. Leigh was learning all she could about horses, because she wanted her very own horse to raise and care for. She had gone to the public library and checked out numerous horse books. Her Mom had told her how she used to ride horses when she was young and had given Leigh her old horse pictures and books of all the different horse breeds. Leigh's favorite horses were "paints" especially the black and white colors with big spots. Her dream was to have her very own "paint horse" that would belong to her someday to love. She just was not sure how it could ever be possible. Her parents told her they did not have the money to buy her a horse of her own.

Could she really have enough faith to believe God could bring her a horse that loved her and accepted her? A horse that was truly all hers? Was this even worth asking God for? Would he even hear her prayer?

PONGO
The Rescue Horse

★ **Chapter 3** ★

Becoming A Horsewoman

That spring for Leigh's birthday her Mom and Dad surprised her with horse riding lessons. She was so excited! They went shopping for riding boots and a safety helmet.

At the horse riding stable, Leigh learned quickly how to properly brush, groom and saddle a horse. She learned how horses communicate with you by the way they move their ears. If they lay their ears back they are scared or upset. When they perk their ears toward you they are paying attention to your commands. Her riding instructor gave her many good tips about communicating with horses.

Leigh felt at home at the riding stable. She began to help out part-time after her homeschool classes, cleaning the stalls, feeding and turning out the horses to their pastures. She was becoming quite the horsewoman. Her horse riding teacher was amazed at how quick she was learning and how hard she would work at the stables. Leigh was taking pride in her work, and could not wait to come home and tell her Mom and Dad all about what she learned that day at the stables.

Soon, Leigh's Mom heard about a local horse rescue farm in need of volunteers to help with their rescues. Her Mom said: "Leigh, let's go see what help they need at the horse rescue - It would be a great way for us to give back to our community." Leigh agreed.

At the horse rescue farm, Leigh and her Mom learned all about the sad lives of the horses and why they needed to be rescued. Some came from auctions where they were abandoned or rejected by their owners, some were abused and had been injured and even near starving to death. If they did not get rescued from the auction in time by a horse rescuer, many would go to the "Last Chance Pen". This was also called a "kill pen". If the horses in these last chance pens did not get saved by horse rescuers they could die, and go to slaughter for meat to other countries. It is very horrible, but true. Thank goodness for the horse rescuers across America! These horse rescue organizations save hundreds of horses from slaughter every year at the auction pens. They bring them home to their safe farms, get them on a good diet of grain, hay and green pasture - good Vet care and within weeks they are looking healthy. With love and patience, they help the abused horses trust people again. Then they are ready to be adopted by a loving family or person who wants to give a rescued horse a long and happy life.

Leigh and her Mom spent hours and hours volunteering at the horse rescue farm, brushing and giving love to the rescue horses. These horses enjoyed receiving the affection and care. Soon, Leigh began teaching the new volunteers on how to care for the rescues. She even put on a horse grooming lesson on the rescue farm's "Volunteer Day". Some families and their children came to learn from Leigh how to be a volunteer at the rescue farm. This was showing Leigh that she could be a leader, people that came to learn were looking up to her.

That year at Christmas time - Leigh had an idea to get her Mom and Dad to take their pickup truck and go and buy a load of fresh hay to bring to the horse rescue. It made Leigh feel happy to give good things, and she was beginning to see there were good people out there who really appreciated her help and her kindness.

Seeing the rescue horses happily munching on the hay that she and her family bought and delivered, proved to her that having a caring heart was a good thing, even if those bullies from school could not see it. She realized then the bullies that she dealt with in school, may have never had the chance to do something good like this, so how could they know what it felt like? Maybe that's why they made fun of her, because what they really needed was an opportunity to be kind. Once they saw how giving kindness made them feel, they would never want to bully anyone again.

That's it! Leigh realized. Bullies don't know how giving kindness feels - they just needed a chance to do something GOOD! Leigh felt at ease in her mind as she finally answered that question for herself. The bullying she got in school and on the bus was not because of her being different. It was because the kids that were bullies did not KNOW how to do good. They just needed to have a chance to do good. It all made sense.

Quietly, she said a quick prayer: "God, I pray for the kids that were mean, and I pray that you give them a chance to be kind and help them see how good it feels, and that they will never want to be mean to anyone again, Amen."

PONGO
The Rescue Horse

★ Chapter 4 ★

Dream Horse

Leigh was doing well with her riding lessons and it was nice working with many different horses over the past year. She enjoyed helping out at the horse rescue, it was very rewarding. But there was still an empty feeling inside her heart - she really wanted her very own horse to love - one that she really connected to. Her Mom could tell she was still struggling with her confidence around people and other kids, and she worried if Leigh could ever start to do more things with kids her age. Leigh had been hurt by the bullies, and she just did not feel ready to go back to public school yet. She wanted to trust that she could make a friend, but she just had a hard time understanding if that could actually happen. She still felt the pain and sting in her mind of the mean words the bullies used to say to her. She was afraid that it could happen again.

Maybe she was just like these rescue horses, Leigh thought. She needed time to heal too, and she needed to feel the love and trust of her very own horse. One that she could work with all by herself and they could grow up together and belong to each other forever. It was hard to get attached to any of the rescue horses she helped, because they would go to new homes soon if they were adopted.

One day while driving home from volunteering at the rescue farm, Leigh was staring out blankly of the passenger side window. Her Mom suddenly said; "Leigh, If you really want a horse to call your own, with faith God will bring it. Let's find a picture of the kind of horse you would want, print it out and post it on your bedroom wall."

Leigh's Mom told her the Bible says that if we write down and post up a picture of our vision, in faith we can ask God for it in Jesus name.   Then we must truly believe God can do the impossible - He will be faithful and make a way for your vision and prayer to come when the time is right.

That evening, Leigh painted a picture of the horse she had dreamed about. A black and white paint horse. She posted it up on her bedroom wall, then said a simple prayer for God to bring her a horse like this - and she would be grateful to God for however He decided to bring it, in Jesus name. Amen

She loved looking at that picture over her bed when she went to sleep every night. Faith was rising up in her heart.

PONGO
The Rescue Horse

★ Chapter 5 ★

Planting A Seed Of Faith

One Sunday while getting ready for church, Leigh's Dad was putting the weekly church offering in the money envelope. Leigh had a few dollars saved up. She saw that Mom and Dad would give money to church and then sometimes say a prayer over it for something they needed. She said, "Dad, can I give an offering to church and pray over it for God to bring my horse?"

Dad explained that our offerings to church are like seeds that you plant in God's kingdom and they will grow into a blessing. If you "name your seed" in faith and ask God to bless it for your need He will. Leigh said, "I only have a few dollars, will that be enough for God to do this?" Her Dad told her that if you give it with all your heart, in faith God will accept it. In God's kingdom He can provide all our needs according to His riches and glory, which has no limits.

So together as a family they put their hands over Leigh's offering of a few dollars, and prayed, "Father, we give thanks for this money and offer it up to You, and we name this seed "Leigh's Horse" that we receive in faith, in Jesus name, Amen" Then she put the money in the collection plate at church. Leigh was wondering what God would do with her money seed - she was feeling very hopeful!

★ Chapter 6 ★

The Last Chance Pen

A few months passed by, then one morning Leigh's Mom saw a horse posted on a social media website that needed to be saved from the auction pen in Pennsylvania. He was a black and white paint! He looked almost exactly like the horse posted on Leigh's wall!

But, the Paint Horse was in the "last chance pen" at the auction. This means that nobody wanted to buy him. He had been rejected by the main auctions, and moved into the "kill pen" where only the meat buyers would get him and he would go to the slaughter house and die within days! Leigh's Mom started to read more about this Paint Horse. He was only three years old! His whole life was in front of him, and he was so pretty!

Mom immediately messaged their local horse rescue, who had also seen the Paint Horse too and was trying to raise the $500 to bail him out and save his life before the "kill buyers" got to him. They said everyone at the horse rescue was getting the word out, His time was short - they had to hurry!

Mom ran with her laptop computer into Leigh's bedroom. Leigh was working on her homeschool classes. "Leigh!" Mom said excitedly. "Stop what you are doing right now you are going to want to see this!"

Leigh could hardly believe her eyes when she saw the Paint Horse's picture on the computer screen. She read all about him and was as astonished as her Mom was on how much he looked like the horse she had posted as her vision on her wall.

Leigh and her parents decided they wanted to help save him right away!

PONGO
The Rescue Horse

★ **Chapter 7** ★

The Paint Horse Is Rescued!

Leigh and her parents donated what they could afford toward bailing out the Paint Horse out of the last chance pen at the auction and asked everyone they knew on social media to donate. The remaining total money was raised within 48 hours! The Paint Horse was saved by paying the $500 "bail" and he was taken out of the kill pen and into a safe holding pen! Praise God! Now they had to get him to their rescue barn in Virginia, the same one that Leigh and her Mom volunteered.

Their local horse rescue arranged for transport to bring the Paint Horse to their rescue farm. He was coming from Pennsylvania, it would be at least a five hour haul down. First, he would need to get his health checked by a Veterinarian, and get approved to be moved out of the state. Everything checked out - he got a clean bill of health and two kind volunteers with horse trailers each hauled him down to Virginia. One halfway to Maryland with an overnight stay and another picking him up and hauling him the rest of the way. Meanwhile, Leigh and her Mom prayed for his safe journey there.

It was late at night when the Paint Horse arrived at the rescue barn in Virginia. He was tired and a bit frightened from all he had just been through, but when he stepped off the trailer at the rescue farm they put him in nice big paddock all to himself! It felt so good for him to stretch his legs and eat fresh green grass after being in those dusty old cramped pens at the auction!

You might be asking yourself, how does a young and very pretty black and white Paint Horse end up in a last chance 'kill pen' at an auction? It's hard to answer that question. But one thing that you can know for sure about this Paint Horse, was that God was doing a very special miracle. His life had an important purpose - for one very special young girl who was faithfully praying and believing God for a horse like him!

That girl was Leigh.

PONGO
The Rescue Horse

★ **Chapter 8** ★

The Meeting Day

The very next morning of the Paint Horse's arrival in Virginia, Leigh and her Mom (and a bag of carrots) went to the rescue farm to go and meet him for the first time! Leigh could hardly sleep all night she was so excited!

When they arrived, they slowly walked up to the pastures behind the rescue barn. The Paint Horse was under a tree along the fence in the shade. You could still see the sticker on his back that had a number and barcode for the last chance pen from the auction. They put these stickers on the auction horses in case the horses are sold by weight for meat. He was a bit skinny, but not starving thank goodness. God was watching over him, because He had a great plan for him and Leigh.

As Leigh and her Mom approached the rescue horse pastures, the other rescues knew they had carrots and started staring curiously at them, some nickering for a treat - but today they were there for one special horse. The Paint Horse.

Leigh slowly walked up to the Paint Horse, while Mom stayed back, recording the special meeting by video on her phone. The Paint Horse walked up to Leigh. She slowly reached out and gently stroked his nose and told him he was safe now and everything was going to be OK. The

Paint Horse loved the carrots and put his head in Leigh's chest as if to say - thank you and I need a hug! When a horse does that for the first time that means he trusts you. Leigh put her arms around him and hugged him back and spoke softly to him. They were instantly bonding and connecting.

This was the beginning of a wonderful new friendship.

★ Chapter 9 ★

A Time To Heal

For the next few weeks Leigh and the Paint Horse spent a lot of time together. They were creating a strong trust and friendship. Most of all they were healing inside from all the hard times they had both been through. Leigh from being bullied by other kids, and the Paint Horse from the cruelty and trauma of the weeks at the auction and last chance pen.

Leigh would walk and talk with the Paint Horse up and down the farm path, brush him and love on him. She gave him his first bath in the wash stall. He was still very afraid of some things like closed spaces and water hoses. Leigh was patient with him and took all new things very slowly. This was so he could get used to the fact that she would not let anything or anyone ever hurt or scare him again.

Leigh was helping him overcome his fears and she was so happy to see she could make a positive difference in this horse's life! She was feeling more confident in herself every time she made good progress with the Paint Horse. This was helping Leigh as much as it was helping the Paint Horse! Each day Leigh would come to the farm and work with the Paint Horse, soon he was following her around without a lead rope. He began to trust in her voice and where she was guiding him to go. When he listened to her commands, such as walk, trot and whoa - she praised him and stroked his neck. He began to see that she was a person he could trust and that would not hurt him, he could follow her lead and be safe and happy.

Then a very special day came. The kind lady who owned the horse rescue farm surprised Leigh with official adoption papers for the Paint Horse. She had been watching the two of them together and went to the horse rescue board members and they all voted that Leigh and the Paint Horse belonged together. That morning they had put a purple ribbon on the Paint Horse and invited Leigh and her parents to come for the official adoption ceremony at the barn! Leigh was so happy and signed the adoption papers. Mom and Dad took pictures and everyone was in tears. Even the Paint Horse seemed to really understand this moment. They now officially belonged to each other! Leigh and her family praised God! God HAD done the impossible! Leigh now has her very own horse who loved her! God had *heard* her prayers!

"I will call him "Pongo Picasso" said Leigh. I think the name fits him, he is here now in Virginia, with me forever safe and sound. He is a Paint Horse so I will name him after one of my favorite painters, too." She said.

The rescue barn offered to board Pongo there at an affordable fee until Leigh's family could bring him home.

Pongo liked his new name. The rest of the summer they kept working on simple training and trust techniques called 'ground work'. Pongo learned to follow Leigh's voice commands. Both Pongo and Leigh looked forward to the cool summer evenings working in the ring. Leigh borrowed ropes, poles and plastic tarps to help Pongo get over his fear of new things around his feet. Soon he was stepping over them with ease.

They had so much fun together. It was a summer Leigh would never forget. Fall was approaching, and the rescue farm was having a Fall Festival to raise money for the farm. Pongo and the other rescues enjoyed horse games like bobbing for apples! Pongo kept dropping his apple - it was slippery! But Leigh would pick it up and feed it to him. All the families at the Fall Festival enjoyed meeting and petting Pongo! He really loved the attention and Leigh was confident to tell everyone how far her horse had come and everything she was teaching him. At the Fall Festival, Leigh and Pongo entered the costume contest dressed up as a painter and horse with a wet paint sign (Get it? "Wet Paint") and they won the costume contest! Leigh was so proud of her new horse! Pongo was having a great time!

Life was good.

PONGO
The Rescue Horse

★ **Chapter 10** ★

Overcoming Fears

Pongo needed to go to school and learn just like Leigh. Even though before his rescue there used to be cruel people in Pongo's life, now he had nice caring people around him who loved and accepted him. Cowboy Ben was a mustang rescue horse trainer. He worked at the rescue farm too. He was an expert at training horses, especially horses that had trust issues, or had been in harsh situations before. Many rescue horses have been through things in their past that nobody knows about. A patient trainer can get a horse past those old painful memories.

Pongo already loved Ben because he fed him, talked to him and gave him treats with the other rescues at the farm. Ben loved Pongo because he was a very kind Cowboy and he saw the potential and good personality in Pongo. Ben was patient with horses that were afraid of new things or had been hurt before. Sometimes animals are afraid of the same things we are. That is why Leigh really understood Pongo. Even though he was an animal, she knew just like a person who had been hurt - you have to learn to trust again, and if you got around the right people and friends who care about you and understand you - you would be OK. Leigh also knew now, that with faith and hope in God - He can put you in a much better situation, all you needed to do was ask and pray, then trust God to do it. Leigh and Pongo had a lot in common. Leigh, Mom and Dad watched safely from the fence while Cowboy Ben slowly put the saddle and bridle on Pongo during training day. It's always important to get a professional trainer to start a new horse under saddle - the trainer will make sure they take all safety precautions for both you and your horse. Pongo was very scared of the different, heavier things on his back, and he tried to buck off the saddle! He looked like a bucking bronco at the rodeo! But soon (and with lots of patience and encouragement), Cowboy Ben got on his back to ride him. He held him very still and then Leigh got up on Pongo's back. She gave him lots of kisses and treats for being a good boy in training, especially his favorite - can you guess - carrots!

Pongo learned that people on your back are not going hurt you, and his trusted friend Leigh was right there to reassure him. He was not scared of the saddle and bridle anymore. It was great day for everyone. For Leigh she learned that building trust with her horse comes with time, patience and giving him daily encouragement. She now understood that these are the things that can lead up to a big breakthrough in overcoming your fears, not just for Pongo - even for herself. Sitting on Pongo's back high up in the saddle - *finally on her own horse* was an amazing accomplishment. Leigh felt very motivated that she could get through more difficult things in her life - and so could Pongo.

Leigh was seeing the rewards of her hard work and patience with Pongo - she was feeling more and more confident in who she was becoming too.

She looked at her horse and he was happy. She watched Cowboy Ben give him a "Good Boy" pat and a couple treats. There was a new sparkle in Pongo's eye. He knew he was a good horse. He was becoming confident in who he was, just like her.

PONGO
The Rescue Horse

★ **Chapter 11** ★

Leigh and Pongo's New Confidence!

Leigh and Pongo had grown so much together over that year. Leigh was confident she could return to public school and she was not afraid of the bullies anymore. Pongo had helped her get over her fears and she had also helped him get over his. If Pongo could do it, she could do it!

Leigh felt stronger in who she was as a person - she had saved a horse and he loved her no matter what! She knew all she needed was faith to get her through any hard times. God answered prayers. He had brought her dream horse! God could do anything and get her through anything.

When she returned to public school after two years of being homeschooled Leigh was not sure if she would run into the kids who had been mean to her in middle school. She was in High School now and everyone had changed so much. She saw the kids who had been the bullies before and they were actually happy to see her! They told her they were sorry for being mean. Leigh forgave them. They were nice to her from that day forward. It seemed like everyone had changed - in a good way!

During her English class each student had to stand up and talk about what they did over the summer with a Power Point. Leigh stood in front of the class and told the story of how she saved Pongo and he saved her with pictures of their progress. The students all clapped at the end of her presentation! She was pleasantly surprised! They all gathered around her after class and wanted to know more about her and Pongo.

Wow - what a difference time could also make on people. Leigh was glad she had taken a few years away from public school to grow in confidence, but at the same time the kids who used to be mean to her had grown too. She thought in her heart that God had answered her prayer about giving these kids a chance to be kind.

Leigh could hardly wait to get off the school bus at the rescue farm to see Pongo. She ran all the way down to his pasture and dug out the carrots she had in the bottom of her backpack for him to munch on. As she looked into his eyes, her heart felt full. She whispered, "Thank You God." She kissed Pongo on the nose as he slobbered carrot pieces on the front of her shirt. But she didn't care. She loved him no matter what.

The weeks went by in High School and Leigh had a lot of homework, but she made sure she went to see Pongo as much as possible.   Sometimes she would bring her homework to the farm and hang out with him.   The guidance counselors at school encouraged Leigh to join a club after school. Leigh loved music, so one day a week she stayed after for Ukulele Club. Slowly but surely Leigh was getting accepted by other students at school. She enjoyed playing the ukulele and she was very good at it. It was fun to play music with the other people who had that same interest. She felt like she could be herself there, and she found that other people felt a lot like her - they just wanted to be accepted for who they were too. Even if they were not popular or in sports. They had a creative side like Leigh. This was so refreshing to her to find a good group. She had no idea so many kids had gone through some of the same things she did. She loved to encourage them.

She was making some new friends. Leigh was no longer shy to do things in groups with other kids. Working at the horse rescue and Pongo had changed her, she was not afraid to be herself anymore. Mom and Dad were so proud to see her new confidence in doing school activities. They would come and pick her up after Ukulele Club. Sometimes a new friend from school would want to come home on the bus with her and hang out with her and Pongo.

Of course Pongo would be his sweet self and everyone who met him fell in love with him too!

Pongo loved the attention. When she would tell other kids his story they could hardly believe it. Who would have thought that this wonderful horse, who was once sent to an auction kill pen to be sold for meat, could have ever had a chance to bring such joy to so many people? This is why it was more and more real every day to Leigh how precious a gift Pongo truly was - and what an amazing thing God had done. Leigh began to look at life in a way she never had before. With hope. Pongo had changed her. Maybe he was meant to show others about hope too?

That spring, Leigh saw a flyer posted up at the local feed store about the upcoming Strawberry Festival and Parade. The high school marching band was going to march in the parade, and many community organizations and businesses were going to build floats. They were asking for locals who had their own horses if they would ride in the parade, too. They had a sign-up sheet posted next to the flyer.

Leigh remembered when she was a little girl, when she came to visit Granny each year and go to the Strawberry Festival - especially to see the horses. It was one of her most favorite memories, it was what began her love for horses. She thought; "I have to ride Pongo in this parade!" It would take some preparation, and more training for her and Pongo, they only had a month to get ready - but with faith and hard work, they could do anything together.

Boldly, Leigh signed her and Pongo up for the Strawberry Festival Parade. Then she ran that afternoon straight to the rescue barn to talk to Cowboy Ben. She found him scooping grain into buckets getting ready to feed all the rescues for the evening feeding time. "Ben! Ben! I have to talk to you right now! It's important!" Leigh exclaimed out of breath as she flew into the feed room in the barn.

Cowboy Ben looked at her like she was one of his wild mustangs that he had to rein in after a full gallop. "What's up girl?" He said in his country drawl.

"Ben, I really *really* need your help." Leigh began. "Pongo and I have a huge opportunity. We could ride in the Strawberry Festival Parade, in front of hundreds of people, loud band music and flashy floats! It would prove that we have both overcome all of our fears and it would mean that we could reach another big goal together!" She could hardly get the words out fast enough.

"Well, hmmm... Cowboy Ben moved his worn, sweat stained cowboy hat up and down at the brim. Then after a pause that seemed like a long time he said, "Ok then. Let's get to work and get you both ready for this parade. You both need to be bomb proof." He chuckled. "Bomb proof?" Asked Leigh. "Yep, I need you both not scared of nothin' and even if a bomb would go off neither you or that horse would even flinch an inch." He replied. Leigh said, "Yes! That's exactly what we need!"

Leigh gave him a big hug and thanked him and ran to get

Pongo out of the pasture. She put on his saddle and bridle and brought him into the ring. Leigh kept her riding helmet and boots in her locker in the tack room at the rescue barn. She never trained without them. Safety first. Leigh called her Mom and told her the news, and she would be late for dinner that evening - she had to get started working with Pongo's parade training right away.

Every afternoon for four weeks, Pongo, Leigh and Cowboy Ben worked and trained and prepared for the parade. They practiced with every crazy thing you could imagine, bouncing big bright beach balls near Pongo as he walked past. They got blow horns and blew them loudly all around him while Leigh rode him down a straight line. They waved flags and shiny streamers all around his head and back. Cowboy Ben even dressed up as a rodeo clown running around Pongo and popping off little firecrackers! Pongo was passing every test.

The volunteers at the rescue barn supported Leigh and Pongo and even brought the other rescue horses to ride in the training ring alongside him to help them prepare. In the parade Leigh would wear a horse rescue shirt and hat and throw free wristbands and candy to the kids with the Horse Rescue website on them. This was so people could donate and offer support. The Rescue Farm would also have a table set up at the Strawberry Festival to collect money donations for the rescue horses needs.

The day before the parade, Cowboy Ben and Leigh wanted to make sure Pongo would load up and ride down easily in the horse trailer. He had not been in a horse trailer since he arrived over a year ago from the auction. This would also allow him get used to the parade route. It's a good thing they practiced because Pongo did not want to get into the trailer. It took an hour and a half to finally get him on there and LOTS of carrots and patience. Cowboy Ben said it was because the last time Pongo was on a trailer he was coming from a scary place, the auction - and he may have thought that he was going back there. This was a good thing to show him that when he gets on the trailer he will be rewarded and always come back to a good place. That was a final bad memory that Leigh had to help Pongo get past. She thought about herself and getting back on the school bus where all the bullies used to be. She totally understood why Pongo needed to get past that fear.

Parade day came. Leigh was up at dawn to bathe Pongo and groom him to perfection. She brushed out his black and white mane until it looked silky and buffed a shine into his coat. Leigh bought him new bright teal blue colored splint boots to go on all four of his legs, and black bell boots for his hoofs. She also got him a bright teal, white, purple and black Navajo design saddle blanket. He looked so handsome! Pongo loaded like a pro into the trailer. It did not even take one carrot to entice him on! Once they got to the parade grounds, Pongo was a perfect gentleman. He even seemed to love the atmosphere of fun, festivities and joy, and neighed a few times while getting ready to march down the parade route. Leigh could hardly believe she was riding her own horse in the Strawberry Festival Parade. It was surreal. She waved to the crowd as Pongo walked proudly down the parade route between the floats and school bands. He looked so beautiful, he was definitely the star he deserved to be. Even Leigh was enjoying the spotlight. She thought, just two years ago she would have never had the courage to do this. But here she was, with her best pal and loyal friend, Pongo - riding together in a parade! In front of hundreds of people! She was so proud of him, she reached down to pat Pongo's neck.

This was a huge goal. They had done it together.

After the parade, Mom and Dad ran over to hug and congratulate Leigh and Pongo. Pongo reached over to nibble on Mom's basket of strawberries she had bought. They all laughed. Dad patted Pongo on his shoulder.

Leigh's heart was filled with joy as she looked at her parents, they truly loved Pongo too. He was part of their family now. "Mom, Dad," Said Leigh. "Thank you for believing in Pongo and I, and thank you for helping me have faith to get through these last few tough years - I am so grateful."

Mom tried to hold back the tears. "We love you sweetheart, and we always believed in you and always will." Then Dad said, "Leigh, God had a plan all the time. He brought us back here to Virginia for a reason. Granny would be so proud of you today."

Yes, Granny would, thought Leigh. She gave Pongo a big hug and stroked his long mane, with tears of joy streaming down her face, and strawberry juice smeared all over Pongo's chin.

"Let's get a picture!" Said Dad. "Yes! we need a family 'selfie' with Pongo!" Mom piped up. Leigh smiled through the tears as Dad held out his phone to take a picture of them all huddled together with Pongo in the middle.

It was the best day ever!

PONGO
The Rescue Horse

★ **Chapter 12** ★

A Family Of Faith

A few weeks after the parade Leigh asked her Mom and Dad if they could build a barn and a fence and bring Pongo home to their own house and land. They had an acre and a half of land next to her house that her Dad had been clearing into a nice grassy field. It was a perfect paddock area for Pongo. It even had space to build a small barn. The rescue barn was kind enough to allow them to board Pongo there until they could afford to bring him home.

It was time. Mom, Dad and Leigh had been praying for a barn and put the picture on the wall of the barn they were believing God in faith for. It had a stall for Pongo and an extra stall for a buddy like a donkey or a miniature horse. Even though they did not have the money needed to build it, they had lots of faith that God would provide it, just like He brought Pongo to them. They sat around the kitchen table before church and prayed over another seed offering and thanked God for their barn and fence in advance, in Jesus name.

That afternoon after church, Dad made himself a sandwich and told Mom and Leigh he would be in his garage next to the house, and needed some quiet time to talk to the Lord. Dad enjoyed working on his old pickup truck or sitting in the rocking chair that used to be Granny's in his garage. Many times he would just sit out there and read his Bible, relaxing and thinking. Dad's garage was where He and God would spend time together and he could get solutions to things that were on his mind. This day, Dad was hoping that God would give him an idea for a way to make some extra money. Money he could put towards building a fence and barn for Pongo to come home. He knew how important it was to Leigh. He loved his daughter and he saw how happy she and Pongo made each other. That horse needed to come home so Leigh could see him every day. He and Leigh had already measured out an area for a fenced in paddock for Pongo on their property. He added up the cost of all the wood and posts and gates, and they would need about two thousand dollars for materials. It was two thousand dollars he did not have right now. Then they would need more to build a small barn before winter.

Dad sat back in the old rocker, finished his sandwich and sipped on some sweet tea. He looked around his garage. He had just finished cleaning and polishing his old pickup truck. Country music played on the radio in the background. He knew he was a blessed man. He had a healthy and happy family, food on the table, a roof over their head. He was a hard working man - always wanting to do right by his family. With all his heart he wanted to build this fence and barn to bring Pongo home and soon. As of right now, only God could give him the answer and the means to do it.

Dad looked up to heaven. "Lord Jesus," Prayed Dad. "Thank you for doing all you have done for my family Lord. Thank you for bringing that horse to help my daughter. We sure love him, and we are grateful to You Lord. We would like to bring this horse Pongo home to us, but we need a fence, Lord. We need a barn. I know nothing is impossible with you Lord, and whatever way you want to bring our fence I am faithful you will do it. If there's something I can do Lord, to make extra money right now, we sowed a seed today in faith at church and I really need an idea to work with You on this Lord. I will wait for Your answer, Thank You Jesus, Amen."

The hours went by, and the sun went down and Dad was still not back in the house. Leigh came into Mom's room where she was catching up on some calls to family. Leigh motioned with her hands and mouthed the words, "Where's Dad?" Mom put up her hand and waved towards the garage. Just as she did that, Dad came charging into the room. "Hey everyone!" Announced Dad. "I need a family meeting here, I have to tell y'all something!" It seemed urgent so Mom got off her call, and she and Leigh met Dad at the kitchen table where they had all their little family meetings. Sitting around the table there was only the three of them, and the dog, Junior and Leigh's new kitten she named Snickers also gathered at the table. Dad had a very excited look on his face.

"Ok family," Started Dad. "I've been thinking about how we can get the money we need to build this fence and barn for Pongo." He started. "I went out to my garage to ask the Lord for an idea, and well He answered me loud and clear!" Dad said gleefully.

Leigh looked at Dad with surprise. Not because he heard from the Lord, but because he actually admitted he heard from the Lord.

Mom was very open about hearing answers from God and sharing them, but Dad was very private about it. He kept to himself about a lot of things, especially his personal walk with God.

"Well what did you hear?" Said Mom leaning forward in

expectation reaching to grab Dad's hand across the table.

Dad continued, "I was sitting there in my garage, all quiet, after I prayed for an idea - and just looking at my truck." He paused. "I was thinking, I sure enjoy cleaning and shining up my truck, and I am pretty good at it."

"We know that Dad." Leigh said with a chuckle as she picked up her new kitten Snickers and sat her in her lap.

"And?" Said Mom expectantly.

"Then I heard it, kinda deep inside me." Said Dad. "Redneck Detailing....." He drew out the words with his hand over his head like a neon sign over the table.

"Redneck Detailing?" Mom looked at him quizzically.

"Yes!" Dad exclaimed. "I am going to start a car and truck cleaning and detailing business right there in my garage! God gave me the perfect idea - it makes total sense!"

"Honey," Mom grabbed both of Dad's hands and looked him in the eyes. "I believe God is taking you right where you are and using exactly what you have at this moment to do this!"

"I know!" Dad said with excitement. "It's gonna work out great. I already have everything I need to get started all in my garage! Thank You Lord!" Dad jumped up from the table. "Now, I need to get some customers quick so we can get the funds together to go order the wood for Pongo's fence. I can charge about $50 to $100 per car for wash, wax and detailing the inside and outside. I figure 20 or so cars and we can do this!" Dad added up out loud.

"I will help you Dad!" Said Leigh. "I am good at cleaning

cars inside!"

"I will make you some flyers!" Mom offered, "We can post them up around town - you know people around here love to support local businesses!"

They all hugged each other - it was a great idea, now they had to get to work and make it happen.

It was perfect timing, Leigh had just started summer vacation from school so all week they worked together to get out flyers and help Dad get customers.

By the following week, Dad was setting appointments for cars to come for cleaning and detailing. It was off to a great start!

The first three weeks, the weather was sunny and dry, Dad was doing great, cars coming in every few days..... then it started to rain. Rain for days and days. The farmers loved it for their corn in the fields, but it was not helping Dad at Redneck Detailing at all. It put business at a standstill, and their hopes for the fence and barn money was not looking too hopeful.

Leigh, Mom and Dad sat in the garage and watched it rain and rain. They were trying not to get discouraged. A few minutes later, they saw their neighbor, Miss Bridgett come down her driveway on her green John Deere Gator to get her mail. She looked up and waved, then rode over to the garage to come chat.

"How are y'all doing with all this rain?" Said Miss Bridgett as she stepped from the Gator briskly and into the garage, holding her mail under her arm.

"Well, not so good." Said Dad. He went on to explain to Miss

Bridgett about his car detailing business and that he was trying to make enough money to build a fence for Leigh's horse to come home. But business was stopped because of the rain. "I can't wash and wax cars then put them right out in the rain." Said Dad as he looked up at the cloudy sky shrugging his shoulders.

"It will have to stop raining eventually, Dad." Said Leigh, trying to encourage him.

"I heard you rescued a horse, Leigh," Said Miss Bridgett. "I think that is fantastic! Tell me about your horse."

Leigh told Miss Bridgett all about Pongo, and she showed her pictures and videos of him on her phone.

"He is a handsome boy!" Said Miss Bridgett. "Seems like he has a great personality, too. I sure miss all my horses. I only have the one now - Jesse - and he's over twenty years old! I got the two mini donkeys to keep him company in the pasture." She pointed back towards her property that joined with theirs.

"Yes," Said Leigh. "It's really good for horses to have a buddy or two. They don't like being alone." Leigh felt a connection with Miss Bridgett as a horsewoman.

"You know," Said Miss Bridgett thoughtfully. "You could bring your fence up to mine out back and see if when you bring Pongo home if my horse Jesse and donkeys will come down and buddy up to him."

"We surely appreciate it, Miss Bridgett." Said Dad. "It would save us on some fence posts too."

"Happy to help!" Replied Miss Bridgett. "I am looking forward to meeting Pongo when he comes home, Leigh.

See y'all later."

Miss Bridgett pulled her raincoat hood over her head, and got back behind the wheel of her John Deere Gator.

Leigh, Mom and Dad all waved and thanked their kind neighbor as she made a break for her house down the lane and past the back pastures while the rain seemed to subside slightly for a few moments.

Dad looked up at the sky and sighed deeply. "I don't think the Lord would have given me this business idea if He did not have a plan to prosper it. I still believe this is gonna work. " Said Dad.

"We are a family of faith." Mom said as she lovingly patted Dad's shoulder. "We are in this together." She continued. "We just need to watch and wait - God loves to surprise us with the unexpected so we know it can only be from Him."

Little did they know that the best surprises were yet to come.

PONGO
The Rescue Horse

★ Chapter 13 ★

Mrs. Ginny Rose

The next week was much better with sunshine finally in the forecast. On the first clear day, Dad started cleaning a car for a very sweet elderly lady from church.

Her name was Mrs. Ginny Rose.

Mrs. Ginny Rose always sat in front of them in church, and Dad loved to chat with her about the old times and history around their area. Mrs. Ginny was filled with information - like a local encyclopedia. She was in her early 90's and loved to talk about the old days.   She was a proper southern lady and drove a huge car, that her late husband, Mr. Fleetwood Rose bought before he passed away five years ago. Even as a widow, Mrs. Ginny Rose kept busy and wanted to keep her car looking new. She was a very traditional southern Virginian lady. She always dressed nicely, with a pretty flowery blouse, pearls, and dress slacks or skirt. She had her hair done once a week at the beauty shop in town and she always was offering you candy or mints from her purse.

Sometimes Leigh and her family would see Mrs. Ginny's car parked at the local senior activity center or in front of the restaurant in town, lunching with her elderly lady friends.

Her light blue Lincoln Continental would be so easy to spot because she had a large American Flag that said "In God We Trust" and "Support Our Veterans" decal on her back window. Mrs. Ginny's husband Fleetwood was a War Veteran, a hero pilot who fought and flew planes in World War Two. They were respected and admired in the community.

Leigh loved Mrs. Ginny Rose too. Leigh was very interested in hearing the old stories about her Granny and Papa's old country store, that they ran for 50 years, before Leigh was even born. Mrs. Ginny Rose had been a good friend of her Granny's. It was respectful to call the older ladies by their 'Miss' or 'Mrs' names - so Leigh and her family, and pretty much everyone who lived around them called her 'Mrs Ginny' for short and out of respect. Maybe it was old fashioned, but the ladies around here still seemed to enjoy being called that, and Leigh was taught to be polite this way.

"Leigh!" Dad called out from the back door of the house. "Come help me finish up Mrs. Ginny's car - I need you to get under the seats with the vacuum."

"Ok Dad - Be right there!" Leigh answered.

Leigh put up the music she was working on learning with her ukelele in her room and ran out to the garage. She was glad the day was finally sunny and warm, maybe Mom could run her up to the rescue barn for a bit to see Pongo.

An hour later, Leigh was finishing up the vacuuming in Mrs. Ginny's car, and Dad was putting polish on her wheels. Just then, Mrs. Ginny pulled up in the driveway with her sister Dottie driving her.

"Hello Mrs. Ginny!" Said Dad. "You are early, we are almost

done with your car, should be about 30 or 40 minutes."

"Oh?" Replied Mrs. Ginny. "Well, do you mind if I wait here for it because Dottie has another appointment to get to."

"Of course we don't mind, Mrs. Ginny." Said Dad. "Let me get you a chair in the shade and Leigh here will keep you company while I finish up."

They set up some lawn chairs under the mimosa tree next to the garage. It smelled so pretty because the puffy pink mimosa flowers were in bloom with butterflies landing on and off them. Leigh and Mrs. Ginny sat down next to each other. "Can I get you something to cold to drink Mrs. Ginny?" Asked Leigh. She wanted to show hospitality to their guest and also Dad's customer.

"Thank you for asking, Leigh." Replied Mrs, Ginny. "I am fine dear. Dottie and I just had a wonderful lunch at that new place in town. You know, the place with the big yellow bee on it? They had the most delicious sweet tea. I have to admit I had the peach pie and ice cream for dessert too!" She giggled.

Leigh smiled. "Mom and I have been thinking of going there to eat, but I have been so busy with school and my horse."

"Your horse?" Mrs. Ginny looked at Leigh wide eyed. "Oh, I love horses! I always wanted one of my own when I was a girl your age!" She said as she grabbed Leigh's hand gently. Leigh looked down at Mrs. Ginny's hand, with perfectly painted nails in soft frosted pink, and she still wore her old worn gold wedding band in memory of her late husband, Fleetwood. It made her miss her Granny who used to hold her hand all the time.

"Yes, I have a horse named Pongo." Replied Leigh. "He is only five years old and a black and white paint. He is a rescue, and I adopted him." Leigh explained.

"That is so good you did that! Horses have such a wonderful nature and you get to grow up together." Said Mrs. Ginny.

"Yes, I am working more on his training to take him on the trails." Leigh explained. "But really I just love to hang out with him, bring him carrots and treats - Pongo makes me laugh all the time."

"You know, Leigh," Mrs. Ginny began. "Many years ago at your Granny and Papa's old store, there used to be a pony named Billyboy that lived out back. He was a character! He would eat tomatoes! I don't think it's good for horses to eat tomatoes, but he ate them no problem!" She laughed gleefully.

"I never heard that story!" Said Leigh. "I love to hear about my great grandparents country store." Leigh leaned in to hear more.

"I have many stories from that old store!" Mrs. Ginny exclaimed as she pointed down the road to where the old store still stood - vacant after many years.

"You would appreciate this story, dear." Mrs Ginny said as she turned in her lawn chair to face Leigh. "Your Granny and Papa were very good people, and helped many folks around here. They ran that store, and never took a vacation. Only closed the store on Sundays. They were hard working and dedicated. They would open the store late at night if someone needed milk for their baby. They did that for me once, when I was out of milk for my little boy - did not even make me pay for it." Her eyes teared up as she remembered her son.

Mrs. Ginny had lost her only son in the Vietnam war. He was a pilot like his dad, Fleetwood. Mrs. Ginny kept a picture of him on her piano in his pilot uniform. Many children around here had taken piano lessons at Mrs. Ginny's house over the years. Leigh had taken a few lessons with Mrs. Ginny but decided she would rather take up the ukulele. It was simple, like a mini guitar and she could teach herself. Leigh thought how amazing that Mrs. Ginny would still give a piano lesson as old as she was. Maybe it was a way for Mrs. Ginny to fill that empty spot in her heart, since she had no grandchildren of her own. Leigh pondered this for a moment. Her heart went out to Mrs. Ginny as she saw her take a tissue out of her purse.

Leigh quickly changed the subject. "Mrs. Ginny, would you like to see a picture of my horse?"

"Oh yes I would!" Mrs. Ginny perked up in her chair. "Let me find my glasses."

Leigh pulled up some pictures of Pongo on her phone.

Mrs. Ginny peered over her bifocals at Leigh's phone screen. "He is a beautiful horse! I can tell he must be a character too!" Mused Mrs. Ginny.

"Thank you, and he is super sweet." Said Leigh. "I hope I can get over to see him today."

"Where do you keep him?" Asked Mrs. Ginny.

"He is still staying at the rescue farm a few miles away. Right now Dad and I are trying to save the money to be able to build a fence here to bring him home." Leigh explained.

"That would be wonderful!" Said Mrs Ginny. "You certainly have the space for a horse to live here happily on your property." Miss Ginny said as she looked over toward the back of the house at the large green acre and a half of land Leigh's Dad had kept neatly mowed.

"Yes Ma'am. We definitely have the area for a pasture for him here," Said Leigh assuredly. "But it's going to cost about two thousand dollars for the fence we need, my Dad and I already measured and have it all figured up. Not sure when we will have the money to be able to buy all the fence supplies. I just hope we can get him home before winter and maybe have enough to build a small barn for him too."

"Have faith dear." Mrs. Ginny said as she put her hand on Leigh's shoulder. "God will bring Pongo home, and He will provide your fence and your barn. He always makes a way - it might not be the way you expect, but it's always on time - and exactly what you need when you need it." Mrs. Ginny said with grandmotherly warmth in her voice.

Leigh thought about the seed offering they had given in church and prayed over weeks ago. Sometimes she forgot that God could be working on things for her and Pongo while they went through daily life. Her hope and faith was sparked up again by Mrs. Ginny's encouragement.

"Yes," Leigh said after a moment. "That's what my Mom always says, too. Pongo is walking proof that God makes a way. We had faith that God would bring a horse for me to love and that loves me, and He did."

"Well there you go!" Said Mrs. Ginny. "If God brought you Pongo, don't you think He can bring a fence and even a barn here for him? Nothing is impossible for God."

"I agree!" Shouted Dad as he walked up behind them, tucking his polishing cloth in his back pocket after wiping the sweat off his brow. "Your car is ready now, Mrs. Ginny."

Both Mrs. Ginny and Leigh jumped, surprised by Dad coming up behind them, since they were in a deep conversation. Leigh hugged Mrs. Ginny and helped her up out of the lawn chair. Mrs Ginny jokingly scolded Dad, "My Gracious! You startled us!"

Dad just smiled. "Your car is as shiny as a new silver dollar Mrs. Ginny! Those ladies at the beauty shop will be able to see their new hair-do's in the reflection of your fenders!" He quipped.

Leigh and Mrs. Ginny laughed. Leigh was so happy to see her Dad taking pride in his work and new business. She waved good-bye to Mrs. Ginny as she headed back into the house.

"Don't forget to give Pongo a pat on the shoulder for me," Said Mrs. Ginny.

"I will!" Said Leigh.

After Mrs. Ginny left happily down the road with her shiny clean car, Mom and Leigh jumped in the pickup and rode over to the rescue barn.

As they pulled into the lane to the rescue farm, Leigh saw Pongo way back in the pasture. He was easy to spot with his white and black markings - even from far away. "Mom." Said Leigh. "Go ahead and park up by the barn, I am going to walk out to the back pasture and just visit Pongo for a few minutes, and then we can head back home."

"Are you sure?" Asked Mom. "Yeah - just give me a few minutes." Answered Leigh.

Leigh walked out to the pasture, Pongo was off grazing by himself. Good, thought Leigh.

When she got close she called his name and he recognized her voice and walked over to her. Leigh patted him on the shoulder and said, "That's from Mrs. Ginny." Then Leigh took a deep breath and looked up at the blue sky. Big fluffy clouds with rays of sun shining over her and Pongo. Perfect. She put her hand around his nose, pulled him close and they both stood very still in the sunny pasture.

Leigh prayed: "Father God, I believe you are going to bring Pongo home to me. I don't know how you are going to do it, or when you are going to do it. I am faithful You will do it. I believe You are bringing the fence and barn we need to bring him home to our house. I trust You God, and Pongo and I thank You in Jesus name, Amen."

Leigh gave Pongo a kiss on the forehead and ran back across the pasture to Mom in the pickup.

"Did you do everything you needed to do with Pongo?" Asked Mom.

"Yup. All good." Said Leigh.

★ Chapter 14 ★

Surprise In The Mail

The next two weeks for Leigh were uneventful, other than helping Dad on a car here and there, going to see Pongo at the rescue barn and playing her ukulele to pass the time. Being faithful and waiting for something big from God can be hard sometimes, but Leigh had said her prayer with Pongo and she was not going to let any doubt creep into her mind. Pongo was coming home. It will happen. God will do it.

Dad was trying to stay faithful too, cars were coming in to clean but not as many or as quickly as he had hoped. Everyone was trying to stay positive and keep each other's spirits up.   Leigh's mom created a social media page for Pongo - she and Leigh went through their pictures and videos and thought it would be a good thing to share Pongo's story encourage others.

Another week went by, still not enough to build the fence, and Dad would have to pay another month's boarding fee for Pongo at the rescue barn.

Even still, Leigh and her family stayed in hope and faith that the fence would be built and Pongo would be home very soon. Leigh remembered Mrs. Ginny's words of encouragement;

"God will bring Pongo home, and He will provide your fence and your barn. He always makes a way - it's always on time and exactly what you need when you need it."

Leigh stayed focused on those words. Mom and Dad kept walking the property where the fence would go and kept seeing things as if they were already 'here' in faith as Mom said the Bible tells us to.

They were a family standing together in faith. It sure takes patience. But Leigh, Mom and Dad all knew without any doubt God would be faithful and do it. Just like Mrs. Ginny said, He brought Pongo, He could surely bring a fence for him to come home. Nothing is to hard for God.

One late afternoon, Leigh's Mom was making dinner and Dad was in town running errands. "Leigh, I have something cooking on the stove, can you run out and get the mail - the mail lady just came by." Mom asked.

"Sure, Mom." Said Leigh. She was barefoot but it was almost all grass to their mailbox, with just a few stones to walk across their driveway, they kind of hurt her feet but she was a country girl now. Country girls were used to going barefoot.

Leigh got to the end of their driveway to the mailbox and leaned over to pull some bills and a couple of advertisements out. She was about to close the lid when she looked inside and saw a light blue envelope. She took it out and looked it over closely as she walked back across the driveway, paying no attention to the stones poking her bare feet.

The envelope was addressed to her, in cursive writing, and had designs on it with old fashioned roses.

Leigh thought, "This is not my birthday, why would I get a card? "

Leigh brought in the mail and laid it down on the kitchen table. She showed Mom the pretty blue envelope.

"Who do you think this is from Mom?" Asked Leigh as Mom came over to the table wiping her hands with a dish towel.

"Hmmmm.... Very pretty handwriting, but I don't recognize it." Said Mom. "Open it and see."

Leigh got a letter opener and carefully sliced the top the of the pretty blue envelope. She delicately pulled out the card that also had pretty roses on it.

She opened the card, it was from Mrs. Ginny.   Inside, there was check for $2000 made out to Leigh's Dad with a memo on the check that said "Pongo's Fence".   There also a handwritten note in the card - Leigh read the note out loud:

Dear Leigh,

Please accept this check as a gift to build the fence to bring your horse home. I had a dream of a horse of my own when I was a young girl like you, too. It warms my heart to see how much you love that horse, and how faithful you and your family have been by rescuing and adopting him. The Lord has been good to me and my late husband and we never had to worry about money. I have no grandchildren of my own, but I know God wants me to bless the children he puts in my path. I enjoyed our conversation a few weeks ago, and I felt the Lord wanted me to do this for you and Pongo. God bless you sweetheart, you are doing a good thing.

With Love,

Mrs. Ginny Rose

PS: What are Pongo's favorite treats? I will come for a visit to meet him in person at your place when he comes home. Maybe we can take one of those 'selfie' pictures on your phone that all the kids are doing. See you all soon!

Leigh looked at her Mom. She was dabbing the tears out of the corners of her eyes with the dish towel. They were both speechless. They stood there for a minute staring at the card, the note and the check for two thousand dollars laying there on the kitchen table. It was an amazing gift.

Just at that moment, Dad came in the door, carrying a grocery bag with some onions and a few other ingredients Mom needed for dinner.

They just looked at him. Mom was still dabbing the tears. Nobody said a word. Then Dad said to Mom, "Have you been cutting onions already? I have not even got them home yet!"

"No, I am not crying because I have been cutting onions, I am crying because of this," Said Mom as she pointed to Mrs. Ginny's card, check and note on the table.

Dad looked over at Leigh. "What is this Leigh, everything OK?" He asked.

"God did it Dad. He did it!! We are getting our fence! Pongo is coming home!" Leigh exclaimed as she picked up the check and handed it to Dad.

"What?" Dad looked at the check in his hands and stared at it. He was speechless too! Then he laid it back on the table and looked at both Leigh and Mom. "This is one of the most generous, kindest things I have ever seen anyone do, in my life. That little horse just tugs on people's hearts." He shook his head in amazement.

"Whooo hoooo!! I am so excited!" Leigh whooped and hollered as she jumped up and down hugging Mom and Dad. Even the dog Junior started barking and jumping and Snickers the kitten started running around the kitchen in celebration with all the excitement.

Then Mom stopped and grabbed their hands, "Hold on, hold on, *whoa* everyone!" Mom spoke loudly like she was reigning in Pongo himself. "I just realized something! This check for $2000 for our fence is sitting here just weeks from the day we wrote and prayed over our seed check to the Church offering to the Lord - on this very same table!"

They all stopped and looked and let that soak in. Leigh's faith rose higher than she have ever felt before.

"Mom," Said Leigh. "It's because God hears our prayers."

"Yes," Said Mom. "Yes He does."

"It all makes sense." Said Dad. "God makes it simpler than we do. You plant a corn seed, you have faith it's gonna grow and get corn to harvest. You plant a seed in God's Kingdom in faith, He's gonna bless you with a harvest of what you are faithful for."

They joined hands and praised and thanked God together.

After dinner, Leigh sat down and wrote a thank you letter to Mrs. Ginny and put a picture of Pongo in there - she knew he was grateful too.

Leigh understood now that God always provides and brings the right people at the right time into your life when you trust Him.

God also loves to give us surprises - so we know it came from Him - just like Mom said.

PONGO
The Rescue Horse

★ **Chapter 15** ★

Bringing Pongo Home

Within a few days, Dad purchased the lumber and started building the new fence and paddock for Pongo on their property. Leigh helped too, hammering in fence rails and helping Dad level up and attach the gates. Mom brought out sandwiches and sweet tea and helped too, making runs to the farm supply store. They bought a water trough, a new feed bucket and even a big red ball toy for Pongo to fling around the paddock for fun.

When the fence was finished, Dad called Cowboy Ben and asked him to pick up Pongo with his horse trailer and haul him safely to their house. Cowboy Ben was happy to help.

The next morning, Cowboy Ben pulled into Leigh's driveway pulling a white horse trailer. Pongo was peeking through the slats from inside the trailer. Leigh could hardly contain her excitement. Mom had tears of happiness and Dad was directing Cowboy Ben to drive back behind the house to the new paddock.

Pongo stepped off the trailer and Leigh was there waiting. She led him happily into his new paddock. He loved it! He galloped all around checking out his new area. Neighing and snorting.

Pongo stuck his head over the gate and nodded it up and

down as if to say, "Yes, I like it here!" Mom got the entire event on video. It was a very special moment. Leigh could hardly believe her very own horse was right here, at her house, in her yard! She could look out her window and there Pongo was looking back at her! She thought about her dream when she first came to Virginia - it came true!

It just took faith. A little faith with patience in God's timing can bring big miracles.

Pongo was home. It was a very interesting journey filled with the unexpected, but he was here and he was happy. Leigh was happy too. She took a 'selfie' picture with Pongo on her phone to keep to remember this day forever. Mom took pictures too and put them on Pongo's social media page. As a family they wanted to share how good God had been to them and for Pongo's story to be an inspiration to others. In the afternoon friends came by to visit and meet Pongo 'in person'.

Mrs. Ginny stopped in to get her 'selfie' picture too and pet him. She gave Pongo some peppermint candies from her purse and of course those became his new favorite treats! Pongo was enjoying his first day at home with so much love from so many good people who helped him get here.

That night while everyone was asleep, Leigh put on her boots and went out the back door quietly. She could not sleep. She had to go see Pongo. The crickets and frogs were chirping in the humid summer night. Leigh walked up to the paddock gate, she could hear Pongo walking across the grass and lightly snorting as he came toward her. She could make out his white spots and big white blaze on his face in the moonlight as he got closer. She stepped inside the gate as he came over and put his head on her chest.

Leigh whispered softly to him. "I love you Pongo. I am so

happy you are here and it's going to be great. Nothing bad can ever happen to you again. You are home. You are home forever."

Pongo put his head over her shoulder as Leigh reached her arms up and hugged his neck. She stepped back and looked into his deep dark eyes as she saw the reflection of the moon.

God had loved her enough to bring this wonderful horse to her and even bring him home to her house. She wondered if Pongo deep inside knew that God loved him too. After all, God had created them both.

They stood there, under the stars in the paddock together, with fireflies blinking across the grass and trees. Leigh could feel Pongo's breath softly on her neck. She put her hand on his heart, she could feel the life in him. The life that could have been cut short back in the kill pen at the auction. But God had a better plan for him and her. Together as they stood there in the warm summer night, Leigh and Pongo were in complete understanding of their Creator and His love for His Creation. It was a divine moment. The night sky was clear and the future was bright for both a special horse and a girl who believed.

Her horse was here. Her heart was full. The future was bright for both of them.

★ Chapter 16 ★

Making New Friends

The next morning, Mom and Dad were out feeding Pongo in his paddock. Miss Bridgett their neighbor came over to meet Pongo. Parking her Gator on the lawn, she walked over to the paddock fence as Pongo came over to greet her.

"I am going to open my back pasture gate and see if my horse Jesse and the donkeys will come down to meet Pongo." Miss Bridgett told Dad. Pongo was nibbling on her sleeve playfully while she pet him over the fence.

"Hey there Miss Bridgett!" Leigh called as she came out the back door of the house. She walked over to them as Miss Bridgett was taking a few treats out of her pocket for Pongo.

"He really likes you Miss Bridgett! He only gets playful like that if he trusts you, and he does not just trust everyone right away." Said Leigh.

"I really like you too, Pongo!" Miss Bridgett said as she gave him a good scratch behind his ear.

"Leigh," Began Miss Bridgett. "I was thinking we could try to get my gang down here to meet Pongo over the fence. If they all get along maybe we can put a gate up between our fences and they can hang out together during the day. It would be alot more pasture for Pongo to graze too."

"That would be awesome Miss Bridgett!" Said Leigh. I know Pongo has been looking over there at your horse, Jesse. He is very social with other horses. There were mini donkeys at the rescue barn that he was buddies with too."

"Let's give it a try, tomorrow." Said Miss Bridgett. "Bring Pongo down my lane about to the halfway gate up closer to where Jesse and the donks are and see if they will meet over that gate."

"Sounds good." Replied Leigh.

The next day, Leigh put Pongo's halter on him and walked him up the lane behind her house right up to the gate where Miss Bridgett's horse Jesse and the donkeys were grazing. She called Miss Bridgett to let her know they were coming so they could arrange the 'close up' meeting.

Pongo neighed loudly over to Jesse. He was excited to meet him. Jesse had only the two mini donkeys Nahbi and Palti for companions in the pasture since Big Mikey died. He had not seen another horse in a while. Jesse was a beautiful red chestnut with a white blaze. He was a retired show jumping horse who had won many ribbons and trophies. Now, aged at 27 years old (80's in human years) Jesse was living out the rest of his days peacefully on Miss Bridgett's farm.

Suddenly, the donkeys came trotting over to the gate. They were excited to meet Pongo! Slowly Jesse came walking over, looking curiously at Pongo. Jesse's shiny coppery coat glistening in the sun, he was looking good for his age.

As the donkeys were poking their noses playfully at Pongo's nose through the gate, Jesse stopped halfway to study the situation at hand. Pongo nickered toward Jesse as if to say 'hello'.

Jesse came over to the gate and sniffed at Pongo with his graying muzzle onto Pongo's black and white spotted one.

Leigh held on to Pongo firmly as Miss Bridgett observed the meeting from the gate as well. Leigh hoped the meeting would be a happy one so they could connect their pastures. Pongo needed pasture buddies too, and alot more room to roam and graze would be a blessing. It's healthy for horses to be with other horses, or even donkeys. They are naturally herd animals and social like people. Sometimes it takes a while for 'new' horse to be accepted into a herd that has already been established for a while. Just like a kid at a new school or class, Pongo had to be patient and willing to build a friendship with Jesse and the donkeys. He was coming into their territory.

Leigh spoke to Pongo in a reassuring tone, and Miss Bridgett did the same for Jesse. It was like a freshman meeting a senior in High School for the first time. Leigh was thinking; "This is just like me coming back into my new high school situation and hoping the kids would accept me!" She mused to herself. She wondered what Pongo was thinking too.

"Sniff, sniff, snort, snort...." were the only sounds coming from Jesse and Pongo as they touched noses at the gate. Then a loud squeal came out of Jesse as he stomped his foot and tossed his head. Pongo stepped back several feet.

"Oh no!" Thought Leigh. "Jesse does not like him!"

"Jesse! Be nice to your new neighbor!" Said Miss Bridgett. "Try again Leigh, Jesse will get used to him, he's just accustomed to being the only horse around here."

Leigh led Pongo back up close to the gate. The white mini donkey Nahbi stuck his head through the lower bars wanting to get closer to Pongo and nibbled on Pongo's chest. Pongo nibbled back on top of Nahbi's head. The donkeys were making friends and playing already. They were quite smaller, about the size of a large dog, but very curious about Pongo.

Jesse the horse was not in a playful mood however. Again, he touched noses with Pongo, sniffed, snorted and squealed - stomping indignantly. This time, Pongo did not move. He stayed at the gate, three more times Jesse did the same thing. Sniffing, snorting, squealing and stomping. Miss Bridgett encouraged Leigh to keep them at the gate to work through the meeting so they could get used to each other, that this was normal horse behavior. Miss Bridgett was more of an experienced horse owner, so Leigh felt a bit better about the situation. But, it did not look like Jesse was too fond of Pongo. Hopefully with time he would be accepted. Leigh thought about her own situations at school, it's so funny how Pongo was going through his own time of acceptance.

Jesse walked back to the pasture and the donkeys followed. Pongo looked after them - longing to go with them too. "That was a start." Said Miss Bridgett. "The big test will be is if they come all the way down the pasture to Pongo's paddock to the fence between our properties on their own. Then we will know that this will work to put them together."

"Ok Miss Bridgett." Said Leigh. She led Pongo back down the lane into his paddock behind her house and bedded him down for the night with hay and fresh water in his trough.

Leigh thought about the kindness of her neighbor Miss Bridgett. It was a generous offer to connect their pastures so Pongo could have more space and some companions. She knew Miss Bridgett really loved horses, hers were so well cared for. Her place was very beautifully kept and she made sure that Jesse did not have to live out his last years alone when she brought the donkeys to her farm. It seemed Miss Bridgett had a truly kind heart for animals, and Leigh was grateful she cared about Pongo's well being. But all this was all based on the fact that Pongo and Jesse could get along. The donkeys were already happy to meet Pongo and wanted to play. Jesse not so much. Leigh hoped that time would change that.

She patted Pongo on the shoulder. "Goodnight buddy. I love you. Hang in there, maybe Jesse will come around. He has to love you, because you are a good guy. He will see, because he is a good guy too." She fluffed Pongo's forelock between his ears and kissed his cheek and went into the house to bed.

Every morning for a week, while Mom, Dad and Leigh we're doing morning feeding for Pongo, Miss Bridgett would ride down the lane in her Gator to Pongo's paddock and visit with him.

"I sure am taking a liking to your boy, here!" Yelled Miss Bridgett, as she rubbed Pongo's nose. "He's got the best personality and he's smart!"

"Thank you Miss Bridgett," Said Leigh. "He likes you too!"

"I sure wish my Jesse and the donks would come down here and connect with him." Miss Bridgett said hopefully. "I left the back gate open to the connecting pasture, so they could walk through - have you seen them down here yet?"

"No, not yet." Answered Leigh. "I see them looking at each other from far away though. I noticed Pongo has made a dusty path on that end of the paddock, seems he is pacing at night to get their attention. Hopefully they will come down here soon."

"Yes, give it time." Said Miss Bridgett. Then she gave Pongo a treat from her pocket. He licked her palm, she gave him a rub on the nose and headed back up the lane on her Gator.

Making new friends and getting accepted by others when you are new isn't always easy.

Even for horses.

PONGO
The Rescue Horse

★ **Chapter 17** ★

Pongo Saved Again

It was a Friday and Leigh had a dentist appointment plus errands to run in town so she hurriedly gave Pongo his morning feed and hay, checked his water and ran in the house to clean up.

When Leigh and Mom returned that afternoon, she noticed Pongo standing under the tree in the paddock, not grazing and his head was hanging down like he was tired. She called to him and he slowly came to the gate, not his usual peppy self. It was a warm day, but he was sweating excessively and very hot - hotter than normal. His nose was very warm, he was breathing hard and his eyes seemed glazed over.

Leigh tried feeding him some of his food and he would not even nibble on it. She became alarmed and texted Mom in the house to come out with some carrots to see if he would eat them.

Mom brought out the carrots and Pongo sniffed at them but would not even take a bite. He was acting very lethargic - he would not even drink water.

Leigh knew something was seriously wrong with her horse.

"Mom, I think Pongo has a colic - we need to call the Vet immediately." Leigh said with urgency. She knew from working at the horse rescue that horses can get a very bad stomach ache called colic. In some cases it could cause a horse to die if you wait too long to get a Veterinarian there to administer medicines. In extreme situations pump their stomachs if the horse ate something toxic.

Mom called the Vet that usually saw Pongo for his checkups. They were closed. It was after hours on a Friday. Leigh was trying not to panic and keep Pongo calm and cool. The best thing to do when a horse gets colic is to walk them slowly and steady and also spray them with cool water to bring down their temperature.

Dad came out to help, he had been busy with cars in the garage and did not notice that Pongo was acting differently. Mom was looking up emergency numbers for large animal Vets in the area that could come quickly. Finally Mom talked to a Vet and he said he could be there in 30 minutes.

Leigh kept walking and talking to Pongo in a calm voice. Hosing him down with cool water and trying to help keep him comfortable. He seemed to be getting weaker and more wobbly when he was walking beside Leigh.

"Please God!" Leigh prayed in her mind. "We have come so far with Pongo, and now this? God, You saved him from the kill pen to bring him here, and now he could die from a colic? Why would this happen? God, You have keep protecting him after all he has been through! I am going to believe You God that You will not allow him to die!" Leigh was trying to keep any negative thoughts out of her mind and stay calm, faithful and focused over Pongo's needs until the Vet arrived.

It was hard to stay brave but she had to do it for Pongo.

While they waited for the Vet, Dad walked around the paddock to see if Pongo had accidentally got into anything that would make him sick.

Dad walked over to the back end of the paddock where he had dug up a wisteria bush that had been growing there before he built the fence. He and Mom had done extensive research to make sure that there were no plants, vines, bushes or trees in the paddock that were poisonous to horses. The wisteria bush was removed before Pongo moved in. It was a pretty bush with purple flowers, but Dad made sure he completely cut it down and chopped out the roots so nothing was left that Pongo could nibble on.

Dad looked closer to where he cut down the wisteria bush. He noticed that Pongo had been pawing in the dirt there with his hoofs. Then he noticed roots sticking up in the dirt. Wisteria roots. Dad bent down and saw that the roots had been dug up and chewed on.

Dad looked over at Leigh walking Pongo carefully at the other end of the paddock. The sun was going down. The Vet was running past 30 minutes. Leigh was trying not to get in a panic, and Pongo was getting weaker and weaker.

Mom's phone rang. It was the Vet. He was 10 minutes away. He told Mom to make sure they kept Pongo walking and awake.

Dad came over to Mom and Leigh and told them about the wisteria roots Pongo had dug up and chewed on in the back corner of the pasture.

"Oh no!" Said Mom. "We worked so hard to make sure that

there was nothing he could get into that was poisonous!"

"I dug up and removed all roots I could find before Pongo got here." Said Dad shaking his head in disbelief. "I would have never thought a horse with a paddock full of green grass to eat would dig down deep in the dirt after some roots."

Just at that moment the Emergency Vet pulled into the driveway with his white utility truck. He put it in park and swiftly jumped out and headed to the paddock.

The Emergency Vet was a stocky man in a khaki shirt and pants with ruffled up hair. He was carrying a case that looked like something similar to what paramedics carry on an emergency ambulance call for people.

Leigh walked Pongo over to the gate. Pongo was very sick, his head was hanging down and his eyelids were drooping. The Vet walked immediately over to him and put his stethoscope onto his neck to take Pongo's vital signs.

Mom, Dad and Leigh gathered around Pongo as the Vet asked questions about Pongo's behavior in the last hour.

Leigh explained that Pongo had no appetite to eat any of his feed or hay, not even his favorite carrots. Also that he would not drink any water. She shared the fact that when she found him an hour before he was standing under the tree sweating badly and breathing hard.

The vet looked around at the new fencing. "Did you just move him in here?" He asked.

"Yes," said Leigh. "He has been here over a week and was doing fine. I know horses can colic if you move them or change their feed. So we made sure he is on the same feed as he was before and he was eating grass and hay too before we moved him."

Dad stepped up to speak to the Vet. "Sir, we want to thank you for coming out here so quickly. I have a strong feeling that Pongo got into some poisonous wisteria roots and ate some, can I show you where they are?"

"Yes, please." Said the Vet. They went over to the back corner of the paddock where the dirt had been pawed up by Pongo and the wisteria roots were sticking up. The Vet looked over the situation and quickly walked back over to Pongo and Leigh.

"Miss!" The Vet instructed Leigh urgently. "Hold on to your horse firmly and get everyone around him to keep him from falling over because I am going to sedate him and treat him for poisoning."

"Poisoning?" Leigh said.

"Yes," The Vet replied. "It's pretty obvious he pawed up that dirt and dug up some of those wisteria roots. That plant is highly toxic to horses, even the roots." The Vet explained. "He is a young horse and curious, they like to chew on things just like little kids. So he must have been trying to paw him up an area that already had some loose dirt - he was attracted to it to make a spot to roll in. Horses like fluffy loose dirt to roll around in, especially in the summer to help with bugs and such."

The Vet stopped explaining as he gave Pongo a shot in his neck. Pongo wobbled and Leigh held on to him stroking his nose and talking softly to him.

"Now," Said the Vet. "Walk him around slowly to keep him

awake while I go get set up."

The Vet walked back to his truck while Dad followed to assist. They came back with a roll of clear tubing, stainless steel buckets and what looked like gallon jugs of medicine.

Mom looked on worriedly and prayed for Pongo. Leigh knew that this was serious. She kept him walking and alert until the Vet got all set up over by the gate.

"Ok. bring him back over here!" Shouted the Vet.

Leigh and Pongo stood quietly while the Vet administered a shot of activated liquid charcoal into Pongo's neck. This would get into his bloodstream and cleanse out any poisons.

Then the Vet mixed the gallons of medications into the clean stainless steel buckets. He took the long clear tubing and put it in through Pongo's nose and pushed it gently down his throat all the way into his stomach.

The sun was almost set and it was getting dark. Time was of the essence. Leigh knew that she would want to be out here with Pongo all night to make sure he made it through this. "Please God let him be OK!" She prayed under her breath.

As the Vet pumped the solution into Pongo's stomach, Pongo stood quietly. He was very sedated with the medications. Leigh was watching him closely to make sure he did not fall over.

The Vet went over to his emergency case and got a flashlight that he strapped across his forehead so he could see what he was doing as he worked on Pongo.

Mom ran back to the garage and grabbed a flashlight so they could see, too.

The Vet explained that he was pumping a solution of activated charcoal mixed with mineral oil and water. The activated charcoal soaked up any poisons in his stomach. The mineral oil and the water was to flush and coat the stomach and intestines.

It seemed like a long time while the Vet was doing this. Finally he removed the hose from Pongo's nose.

"Now Miss," Instructed the Vet to Leigh. "Walk him until he poops and pees. That way we know that he is eliminating the poisons from his body."

Leigh walked Pongo slowly around the paddock, it was now completely dark outside. The Vet was cleaning his equipment up and talking with Mom. Dad had grabbed a shovel from the garage and was digging up and throwing out every last root he could find from the poisonous wisteria. This time he went really, really deep in the dirt.

The Vet explained to Mom that they must keep Pongo walking until he poops and pees, then try to get him to drink some fresh water. If he seems hot, cool him down with a hose and repeat this process for the next few hours until you see his energy come back and he perks back up.

Mom thanked the Vet and he left in his white utility truck, as Leigh saw his headlights pulling out of her driveway she knew she and Pongo would have a long night. She did not care, she just wanted her horse to get better.

Dad came over and walked beside Leigh and Pongo. He was feeling really bad and blaming himself about Pongo getting sick. "Leigh, I am so sorry sweetheart." Said Dad. "I love Pongo too and I thought those darn roots were all dug up, but I guess not. I tried my best to make this paddock safe for him."

"Dad, don't beat yourself up." Replied Leigh. "He's going to be fine."

Just that moment, Pongo stopped and did a great big poop.

"Yes! He pooped!' Leigh gave a sigh of relief. She had never been more happy to see a pile of horse manure in her life.

Dad was happy too and yelled over to Mom to bring the manure bucket and scoop.

"Yay!! Pongo pooped!" Mom was running across the paddock to them trying to hold a flashlight, the poop scooper and drag the manure bucket all at once. "The Vet said that is a good sign!" Mom exclaimed.

"Let's see if he will take a drink of water." Said Leigh. She walked Pongo over to his trough. Leigh splashed some water up on Pongo's lips. He started licking the splashes, then slowly put his mouth in the water and took several big sips.

"Good boy!" Leigh encouraged him to keep drinking. Pongo raised his head up and perked his ears and looked around - his eyes were not glassy anymore and he was getting his energy back.

"Phew!" Dad wiped his brow in relief. "Looks like our boy is gonna make it! Thank the Lord!"

"Yes! Thank the Lord!" Mom repeated.

Leigh walked Pongo for another lap around the paddock, his steps got quicker and she could feel his energy coming back on the end of the lead rope. She made another lap and he pooped again. Another good sign. All the toxins and poisons where coming out of him. She could see him coming back to his old self.

She walked him back over to the water, he took more big drinks. This time splashing his nose in the water a little bit like he always does. Her horse was coming back. Pongo would live! He was going to make it! Relief started to wash over Leigh.

She went to take another lap with him around the paddock. Mom came over and said; "Leigh, let me walk him for a bit, you go take a break - you look tired, sweetheart."

Leigh handed Mom the lead rope, and walked over to the picnic table in the backyard overseeing the paddock. Dad had brought her out a cold bottle of water. She took a sip. Dad put his arm around her and told her he was proud of how brave she was for Pongo tonight. Leigh looked up at the sky into the starry night, as tears streamed down her face as she whispered: "Thank You God, You saved my horse again."

That night, Mom, Dad and Leigh took turns all night walking Pongo around the paddock. The Vet said he would not be completely out of the colic until he had pooped and peed several times, getting everything out of his system.

It was a long night. They were out there until daybreak. The Vet had called Mom at midnight to check on Pongo. He said if Pongo kept perking up they could give him some hay in the morning, but no feed or treats.

As Pongo munched on the hay, the sun was rising. His appetite was back. He was past the worst of the colic and recovering. Leigh and her parents went in the house to rest and get some breakfast. They were exhausted.

Leigh took a quick shower and laid down in her bed for a few hours to get some sleep. She woke up to her Mom shaking her. "Leigh!" Wake up! Come out to the paddock, come quickly you have to see this!"

Leigh jumped out of bed in her 'sleep' shorts and t-shirt and ran outside.

She could hardly believe her eyes. There was Pongo down at the back fence that connected to Miss Bridgett's pasture. On the other side of the fence were the two donkeys and Jesse the horse. Jesse and Pongo had their heads over the fence rubbing noses! Nobody was stomping or squealing - this was a friendly meetup!

"Well, would you look at that!" Chuckled Dad. "Pongo's neighbors finally decided to come down for a visit this morning!"

"Oh my goodness! They like each other!" Mom started to walk over closer wanting to take a picture with her phone.

"Mom, hold on." Said Leigh. "Let's wait and just let them connect without us interfering and see how long they stay down here."

"Okay." Said Mom, "I will go call Miss Bridgett and let her know that they finally came down to visit with him on their own, and Jesse is being friendly with Pongo."

Leigh observed Jesse and Pongo from the backyard picnic table. The two of them were reaching as far as they could over the fence, rubbing and scratching on each other's necks. That is a very good sign for horses - it's a form of friendship behavior. They spent at least an hour at the fence getting to know each other.

Leigh breathed a huge sigh of relief. Jesse had come down on his own to spend time with Pongo. This was huge. He did come around! Pongo had a new friend! What a beautiful surprise to wake up to after such a difficult night.

Mom came over beside Leigh. She was thinking the same thing. "Leigh," Mom said softly. "This reminds me of that verse in the Bible; There may be tears in the night, but joy comes in the morning." Wow, yes. Thought Leigh. How quickly God can turn things around for good.

What Leigh did not know was that it was going to get even better than this.

PONGO

The Rescue Horse

★ Chapter 18 ★

Miss Bridgett's Offer

The next few days Pongo was making steady improvements, and each morning after feeding time, Jesse and the donkeys were making a daily visit to him.

The following Friday, a week after Pongo's colic episode, Miss Bridgett came down the lane in her Gator. Pongo was eating his breakfast and Leigh, Mom and Dad were cleaning the paddock.

"Hey, Miss Bridgett." Greeted Leigh.

"Morning!" Replied Miss Bridgett. "Looks like Pongo is feeling much better!"

"Yes, he is making a full recovery." Said Leigh.

"I see my gang is heading down here to visit him again," Said Miss Bridgett as she pointed over to her pasture at Jesse and the donkeys on their way down to Pongo's fence.

"This is a good sign, Leigh. They all like each other. I can tell the donk's want to play and run with him, too." Said Miss Bridgett.

"I know!" Leigh said cheerfully. "How cute would it be for

Pongo and the donkeys to run around together? Your little white one Nahbi keeps jumping up at the fence rearing his legs at Pongo like c'mon let's go play!" Leigh quipped.

"Listen, I have been thinking," Said Miss Bridgett. "I have an idea and I want to talk to y'all about it."

Everyone gathered around Miss Bridgett's Gator.

"I can see that Pongo is a really nice horse with a great disposition." Began Miss Bridgett. "I like him and my gang has accepted him, too...." She paused.

Leigh, Mom and Dad were listening intently. Not sure what she was going to say next.

Miss Bridgett continued. "Let's just bring Pongo over to my barn and give him Big Mikey's old stall. He would have the full pasture too and we could try putting everyone together."

Leigh, Mom and Dad all stood there in shock.

"Miss Bridgett, That is a very generous offer." Began Dad. "Are you sure?"

"I'm sure." Said Miss Bridgett matter of factly. "Jesse is a very old horse. He probably only has a few more years of life, and the donks are still pretty young. With Pongo only being five years old this would be good for them to have another horse just in case Jesse goes. Pongo would have pasture mates too."   Miss Bridgett looked over at her beautiful chestnut horse Jesse fondly as he came over to the fence to greet Pongo.

"Yes, I think it would be good for everyone." Said Mom. "Leigh could easily walk up there to be with Pongo anytime and we can still see him from the house, right Leigh?"

Leigh was still in a state of shock. She was blown away by Miss Bridgett's offer. She thought about her first friend when she moved here years ago, Big Mikey the old bay horse - he had given her so much comfort and how sad she was when he died. Now, her very own horse was going to move into his old stall and pasture. The same place where she had spent hours and hours with Big Mikey, dreaming of her own horse someday. It almost seemed like she was standing in a dream at that moment.

"Right, Leigh?" Mom repeated and nudged her with her elbow.

"Yes, yes, right...." Said Leigh, She was still standing there amazed at what was happening. Then she got her composure. "Thank you so much, Miss Bridgett. This would be awesome for Pongo and all of us!"

"Then it's settled." Said Miss Bridgett. "Let's plan on moving him up to my barn on Sunday, that gives me a day or two to prepare for him. I will come with the Gator to move up his feed and hay and whatever else you want to bring with him." Miss Bridgett continued. "Oh and if you want to use the big riding ring for his training you can use that too. Heck, we might as well put it to good use! I really think he's a special horse."

Mom and Leigh looked at each other in excitement. This was unbelievable.

"Miss Bridgett, I know you can't do this all for free, what can we pay you for this?" Asked Dad.

"Just cover some expenses for electricity, water and bedding - and I might need you to take care and feed my

94

gang some days." Miss Bridgett answered. "This would be a big help because I have been wanting to take a vacation! You know, I might need a horse and donkey sitter - those can be hard to find and y'all are right here next door!" She laughed.

"You got it!" Said Dad.

"See you all Sunday, you too Pongo!" Miss Bridgett waved as she drove back up the lane on her Gator.

Leigh stood there looking at Mom and Dad. "Are you Ok with all this Leigh?" Asked Mom.

"Yes! I am just so surprised." Answered Leigh. "This is a huge thing. I mean Pongo will have his own stall and I can still be close by, walking distance. Dad, Can we still put in a gate, for Pongo come into this paddock too any time he wants?"

"Sure Leigh," Said Dad. "This is all going to help a lot. Now we know Pongo will have a barn to stay in before winter. We were praying for a barn and God brought it in a way we never expected."

God did bring the barn for Pongo. It hit Leigh all of a sudden. He brought it. A beautiful barn. They did not have to save money or build it themselves. God knew all the time. It was the same barn that she admired from her backyard for years, the same barn that she and Granny used to enjoy from the view in the sliding glass window in the kitchen when she was just a tiny little girl. It all came together. God needed to get Pongo there so he could meet Miss Bridgett because she was part of his journey too.

Leigh was realizing that's how God works. He blesses you in ways you would never expect, and he fills the empty spaces in people's hearts. Leigh thought about the card she sent Miss Bridgett when Big Mikey died, and how Mom said Miss Bridgett was very sad too. She realized now how that could have felt because she almost lost her own horse a week ago when he was so sick. Leigh hoped that Pongo would always be a blessing to everyone around him, especially for Miss Bridgett.

Pongo brought Miss Bridgett joy too, and now new life to her barn and her beloved animals. His life had even more purpose.

★ Chapter 19 ★

Pongo Gets A Barn

Sunday came, and as soon as they got home from church, they heard Miss Bridgett pull up in the Gator. She was prepared for Pongo's move to her barn. Mom, Dad and Leigh ate a quick lunch and went out to get Pongo for his big move.

They put on his halter, clipped on his lead rope and led him down the lane to Miss Bridgett's barn. Pongo was excited! He knew something special was happening. He pranced up the lane with his ears perked up and his head held high. The donkeys came trotting up along the fence and Jesse and Pongo started neighing to each other.

Miss Bridgett led the way in the Gator, loaded up with Pongo's storage trunk, his grooming tools, his big feed storage can, and his red ball toy.

As they arrived at the barn, Pongo easily walked into Big Mikey's old stall and made himself at home. It was like he had been there for years!

Miss Bridgett kept the gate closed between the two runs outside the horse stalls while her gang came over to investigate Pongo being there.

Everyone was excited and happy. Pongo and Jesse kept trotting back and forth for a few minutes and stopping to nibble at each other over the fence and rub noses. After about 30 minutes, Miss Bridgett gave the OK to open the gate and for Pongo to come into Jesse and the donkey's pasture.

The next thing was absolutely comical as Pongo and Nahbi the mini donkey ran and played and bucked and reared up and down the pasture. They had been waiting for this! Jesse looked on as he was old and did not do the galloping and bucking thing anymore. However, he seemed amused watching the scene as the little white donkey chased Pongo around like a puppy dog. Pongo loved it and ran as fast as he could up and down the long green lush pasture with Nahbi in pursuit.

Miss Bridgett was loving it too. They were all having a blast together.

Mom was taking videos on her phone and Dad was filling up Pongo's water trough on his side of the pasture run.

For now they would be together in one pasture during the day, and at night they would go in their own stalls in the barn.

Leigh was so happy to see Pongo quickly adjusting so well. Even the barn cats seemed to like all the new action happening at the barn! They came out to check everything out and get petted by Leigh and her parents.

Leigh bedded down and fed Pongo for the night and closed him in the stall. He was very cozy with nice soft bedding and a fan to keep him cool. Miss Bridgett went over the barn rules, to keep things swept up, and showed them where everything is, like storage and lights if they had to come there at night. Leigh, Mom and Dad wanted to make sure they followed the rules and respected Miss Bridgett's barn. Miss Bridgett made them all feel at home, too.

The next morning, Leigh walked up the lane to feed Pongo at the barn. Dad and Mom went to go and buy some extra hay to store in the barn for Pongo. When they got back to the barn they had a surprise for Leigh.

Dad had a large wooden sign with Pongo's name on it.

"Leigh," Dad said. "I made this sign a while ago and I was saving it for when we built our barn. I thought it would make a good Christmas present for you and Pongo. I feel this is a perfect time to give it to you both, after all it's close to the same date you adopted Pongo two years ago. Sort of a Birthday Present for Pongo." Dad held out the sign to Leigh proudly.

It was a beautiful sign. Leigh thought about it for a minute. She pulled her phone out of her back pocket to check the date. It was July 29th. Today was the exact date she had officially adopted Pongo! It was their two year anniversary! Wow. What an amazing two years it had been. How much they had both grown. They had healed each other and overcome the bad memories and pain from their past. Many wonderful people and blessings had come into their lives since that day. She thought back to the first day she met Pongo, when he came from the horrible experience of the auction pens, and she was trying to get over her own horrible experience from all the bullying. How alike she and Pongo were in so many ways. They needed each other. They gave each other hope. It was miracle after miracle since the day she put up that picture of her dream horse over her bed and believed God would bring him. Now there he was right here and Dad was putting up his name over his stall - over his 'bed'. They had come full circle.

Dad stacked the hay bales next to Pongo's stall and Miss Bridgett brought over a ladder. Dad attached Pongo's new sign with his name on it over his stall door. It was complete. It was that final touch in this amazing journey. Pongo was in his barn, his own stall - safe and sound. He was in his happy place. He was home, for good.

Leigh, Mom, Dad, and Miss Bridgett all stepped back to see how nice it looked. The barn cat jumped up on the hay bales and rubbed her head up against Pongo's nose. He licked her on the head giving her a big wet kiss. Everyone laughed.

Pongo looked out of his stall door at his loved ones - his forever family - standing around him. He was enjoying life. It was perfect. Leigh could not stop smiling, and as she looked over at her sweet and beautiful paint horse, she was convinced he was smiling too.

Leigh thought back about the day she moved to Virginia a few years ago, riding up the country roads wondering why God had brought her here.

Now, she realized it was to rescue a very special horse, that rescued her in return.

Wow! God is so good. Leigh was feeling very grateful at that moment. She knew now, because of what she and Pongo had been through and overcome together, they never had to fear - they could do anything they dreamed of.

God answers prayers. Faith can bring miracles. There was no longer any doubt in Leigh's mind. Her miracle was right in front of her, and he was a sweet paint horse named

Pongo.

PONGO
The Rescue Horse

YOU ARE NOT REJECTED - YOU ARE RESCUED!

Sometimes we feel rejected. We want others to like us and be our friend. Many times people make bad choices and are unkind and act mean to us instead. It does not mean you are not loved. Just like Pongo the Paint Horse, he might have thought he was rejected and unloved when nobody wanted him and he was sent to the last chance pen.

But there was a young girl who was ready to love him, and accept him. God knew what was in Leigh's heart and her dream and provided a way for Leigh to rescue Pongo and give him a good life. Pongo helped Leigh feel loved and accepted too. Leigh realized that they gave hope and happiness to each other, and she could be herself no matter what people thought.

This is how God the Father feels about us. He sent His son Jesus to rescue us and give us hope. Jesus is our Savior and takes our hurts and loneliness away. Many times God will use animals and pets to show how much He and His Son Jesus loves us. The Bible says when we ask God for help with our needs, if we ask in His Son Jesus name it will be done for us. Just like Mom and Dad wanted to do everything they could for Leigh - God is a loving Father too. We are also adopted sons and daughters of God when we believe in His Son Jesus Christ.

You are never rejected, no matter what you are loved and accepted by God who created you and created all the animals. He wants to show you He is real by answering your prayers and giving you a wonderful future. Just like Leigh gave to Pongo. Just have faith. God is moved by our faith and wants to give us good gifts if we believe He will.

God tells us in the Bible that He will rescue us:

"I have made you, I will carry you, I will sustain you, and I will rescue you." - Isaiah 46:4

FAITH CHALLENGE FOR KIDS AND FAMILIES

Is there something in your heart that you are believing God will bring into your life? You can activate your faith and vision with these steps and believing God's promises from His Word:

Create Your Vision: "And the Lord answered me; "Write the vision, and make it plain on tablets, that he who runs may read it. For the vision awaits an appointed time; it testifies of the end, and will not lie. Though it lingers, wait for it, since it will surely come and not delay." - Habakkuk 2:2-3

Ask In Faith: "Truly, truly, I tell you, whatever you ask the Father in My name, He will give you." - John 16:23

Name Your Seed: "So is my word that goes out from my mouth: It will not return to me empty, but will accomplish what I desire and achieve the purpose for which I sent it." - Isaiah 55:11

God Wants To Give You Good Gifts: "Every good gift and every perfect gift is from above, and cometh down from the Father of lights, with whom is no variableness, neither shadow of turning." - James 1:17

Don't Give Up: "And let us not grow weary of doing good, for in due season we will reap, if we do not give up. So then, as we have opportunity, let us do good to everyone, and especially to those who are of the household of faith." - Galatians 6:9-10

Expect Good Things To Come: "And we know that all things work together for good to them that love God, to them who are the called according to his purpose." - Romans 8:28

Ten Steps To Receiving Your Vision In Faith:

1.) **Put up your vision up on the wall**
2.) **Ask God for it in prayer in Jesus name**
3.) **Plant a 'seed' into God's Kingdom**
4.) **Thank Jesus for it in advance**
5.) **Wait for God to bring it at the right time**
6.) **Stay faithful and believe**
7.) **Be expectant for the opportunities**
8.) **Take action on the opportunity**
9.) **Be open to God's direction**
10.) **Praise God for His Goodness!**

When you give with your heart, you are planting a seed of goodness that will come back to bless you. For example when Leigh gave of her time to volunteer and money to buy hay for the horse rescue, a blessing came back for Leigh for all she needed to care for Pongo. When you 'name a seed' to plant in God's Kingdom for your prayer and need - God honors that seed in which you name it. Just like if you plant corn seeds, you harvest corn, not daisies. God's Word does not return void or empty, it will always be fulfilled for which they are sent or 'planted' in faith. God is always faithful to His Word.

PONGO
The Rescue Horse

PARENTS: HOW TO HELP A CHILD BEING BULLIED

If your child is being bullied, it deeply effects their confidence in themselves. Many bullied children will keep trying to make friends with the bullies because they don't understand why the kids are being mean, and why they are being picked on or singled out. This just makes the bullied child try to put all their self worth in if the other kids like them or not. Sharing this story of Pongo and Leigh can help them understand that God loves them and can get them excited about their future!

Create a way for your child to work on a vision for the things they love away from where the bullies are. Encourage them to act out on their vision, build their faith and excitement for what God can do for them. The Bible says the people without vision, perish. (Proverbs 29:18) Activating a child's vision is activating their faith. Jesus said even with a tiny bit of faith - as small as a mustard seed, we can move mountains. Faith is hope, hope is faith. Our children need something to hope for. This changed Leigh's focus from the bullies and the pain of being lonely to something else that she had a deep interest in. It gave her a way to look ahead and not on the past.

Give children a way to tangibly see God operating in their life. Encourage them to go and help in the community where they will see the fruits of their efforts. As parents, come together with your child or children and believe God in faith for something special for your family. If your child is struggling with faith, you can show that you have enough faith for both of you. Your actions in faith will show God is a loving Father. Children learn by example. Everyone's faith will grow together! This will show the child that their self-worth comes from God and their purpose. They will learn not to base their value on the acceptance of other kids. Of course we highly suggest volunteering at horse rescues - horses are natural therapists and the kids can identify with their stories.

How to deal with bullies - 5 tips for kids:

Bullying is a very real and painful situation for a child or a teen. Many times as parents we are not sure how to help our child deal with bullying. Here is an exercise you can give your child to do to help them with some daily solutions they can implement. Ask them to write down five things they can do to deal with bullying. Tell them to keep the list in their pocket or on their phones to remind them. This will empower them and help them realize that they are not helpless against this - they are pro-active. Here is an example, that Landry (Leigh, Pongo's real-life owner) used to help her cope with getting bullied during school.

1. Follow the Golden Rule - Treat others as you would want to treat yourself (Matthew 7:12)

2. Trust your instincts (Get out of a bad situation quickly - walk away!)

3. Set clear personal boundaries (Say: "No I am sorry but you cannot talk to me like that!")

4. Tell the right person (Go quickly to a teacher, your principal or your parents.)

5. Be confident in who you are! (Know that God loves you and watches over you. The bullies have no power over God's good plan for you!)

PONGO
The Rescue Horse

SUPPORTING HORSE RESCUE

Horses are God's creation and among our noblest creatures. In the Bible (Genesis 2:20), God tells Adam to care for His creation on earth. God does not want animals to be treated cruelly. Adam gave all the animals names and loved them according to obedience to God.

It says in Proverbs 12:10: *"A righteous man has kind regard for the life of his animal, But the compassion of the wicked is cruel."* If we are to be righteous in the eyes of God we must have compassion for animals.

Friends, We want to encourage you to support a local horse rescue in your community. Without the help of our local horse rescue, we would not have been able to save Pongo and adopt him. When we rescue an animal from cruelty and abuse, we are doing what God has called us to do.

We are grateful for the tireless work of horse rescue and adoption organizations and many need funding so they can rescue more horses from the auction kill pens across America.

Many horse rescue farms also offer therapy and confidence building programs for children and teens. Before you rescue or adopt a horse, take the time to volunteer at a local horse rescue farm, and learn all you can. So many of these horses just need love and attention, it's a rewarding time for all!

✫PONGO✫
The Rescue Horse

About The Author: Annamarie Strawhand

Annamarie Strawhand is a Christian author, mentor, ministry leader, speaker and host of Life in The Faith Lane TV on YouTube. She is passionate about helping God's people discover their gifts and come into their true calling and divine purpose. She believes her calling is to promote God's goodness, at the same time mentor and teach people to experience His goodness beyond their wildest dreams in every aspect of their lives. Annamarie lives in the country in the southern region of Virginia Beach, Virginia with her husband Michael and daughter Landry Leigh. They have a dog named Junior, a cat named Snickers and of course, a paint rescue horse named Pongo. Learn more on Annamarie's website: www.annamariestrawhand.com

Photo Credit: Gina Marie Johnson @islandmonkeyphotography

About The Illustrator: Nick Lewis

Nick Lewis is an illustrator and graphic artist living in Philadelphia, PA. Nick's passion for art has enabled him to take a message that were once only in the mind as 'words' and give it life as an 'image that engages our imaginations. Nick believes that art is first a gift from God and that when created with purity, it directs people back to their loving creator. Originally from MS, he and his wife, Susan, along with their two boys, Eli and Noah, moved to Pennsylvania to join Watershed Church as Church Planting Team Members. As a business owner, Nick hopes to continue serving the city of Philadelphia by creating quality artwork while utilizing the platform for the good and growth of God's Kingdom. See Nick's work at www.nicklewisartanddesign.com

Photo Credit: Christy McMahon @studioluminoso

The real Pongo with his best friend and owner,

Landry 'Leigh' Strawhand

This book is dedicated to all who have been abused, bullied or felt overlooked, unloved, unaccepted and rejected. God has a great plan for you and loves you very much.

"You Are Not Rejected - You Are Rescued."

"For I know the plans I have for you," declares the LORD, "plans to prosper you and not to harm you, plans to give you hope and a future." - Jeremiah 29:11

A portion of the proceeds from this book, "Pongo The Rescue Horse" go to supporting horse rescue, and helping children and teens overcome the effects of bullying through our ministry. Help us spread the message of God's love and faithfulness through Pongo's true story.

Learn more on the Official Website for Pongo The Rescue Horse: www.pongotherescuehorse.com

<u>DISCLAIMER:</u>

This book, "Pongo The Rescue Horse" is based on true events, real people and their animals. The author would like to thank everyone who has willingly and lovingly wanted to be a part of this story. This book is a personal memoir and meant to inspire and teach. It reflects the author's present recollections of experiences over time in her family and those in her local community. This story is inspired by the actual accounts of individuals and events surrounding Pongo, a horse adopted by the daughter of the author and their journey of faith and healing. Some names and places have been changed, some events have been compressed, and some dialogue has been recreated. Similarities to any persons, animals, (living or deceased) places or events outside of this story are purely coincidental.

IN MEMORY OF MR. GREG WORLEY

Cowboy, Horse Trainer and Friend of God

1959-2018

"Give me some time with an unbeliever in a round pen with a horse, and I can win 'em right there for Jesus Christ." - Greg Worley

IN MEMORY OF MIKEY THE HORSE

"Our Friend"

Enjoy the lush green pastures in Heaven, Mikey, we miss you.

We dedicate this book to the Holy Spirit - Who hovers over all His creation.

Thank You Father God for making this all possible in the name of Your Son Jesus Christ our Savior, Amen.